THE SOCIAL PHILOSPHY OF MAHATMA GANDHI

About the Author

Dr. K.S. BHARATHI did his Master's Degree in Gandhian Thought, Peace-Science, Economics, Political Science and History. He also did Postgraduate Diplomas in Politics, Public Administration, Population Dynamics, Gandhian Thought, Tourism, Telugu and Business Management. He has contributed some articles in learned journals in India and abroad, He is the author of : Foundations of Gandhian Thought, Gandhi and Humanity, Socio-Religious Thoughts of Mahatma Gandhi, Gandhi and Ideology of Satyagraha, The Philosophy of Sarvodaya, Satyagraha of Mahatma Gandhi and Gandhi and Nehru. At Present, he is the Head of the Postgraduate Department of Gandhian Thought of Nagpur University, He is a member of the Academic Council, member of the Senate, member of the Board of Studies of Gandhian Thought, member of the Faculty of Social Sciences, member of the Doctoral Research Committee and member of the B.U.T.R. of Nagpur University.

Gandhian Studies and Peace Research Series-4

THE SOCIAL PHILOSPHY OF MAHATMA GANDHI

K.S. Bharathi

CONCEPT PUBLISHING COMPANY PVT. LTD.
NEW DELHI-110059

ISBN : 978-81-7022-362-7

Edition 2020

Published and Printed by

Concept
Since 1974

Concept Publishing Company Pvt. Ltd.
A/15-16, Commercial Block, Mohan Garden,
New Delhi-110059 (INDIA)
T: +91 11 25351460, +91 11 25351794
E: publishing@conceptpub.com, *W*: www.conceptpub.com

Cataloging in Publication Data--Courtesy: D.K. Agencies (P) Ltd. <docinfo@dkagencies.com>

Bharathi, K. S., author.
The social philosophy of Mahatma Gandhi / K.S. Bharathi.
pages cm. -- (Gandhian studies and peace research series ; 4)
Reprint. Originally published: 1991.
Includes bibliographical references and index.
ISBN 9788170223627

1. Gandhi, Mahatma, 1869-1948--Political and social views. 2. Social sciences--Philosophy. 3. India--Social conditions. I. Title. II. Series: Gandhian studies and peace research series ; 4.

LCC DS481.G3B43 2020 | DDC 954 23

TO
MY PARENTS
SWAMY
KUMARIBAI

PREFACE

THERE ARE many valuable books on Gandhian Thought. But, hardly any one of them offers a comprehensive discussion of Gandhiji as a social thinker. This work seeks to provide a comprehensive exposition of Gandhi as a social thinker and also shows that Gandhian ideas do have a rational philosophical validity.

The constructive work aims at removing disabilities of the people at the social, political, economic and spiritual levels. Wars and conflicts arise, often from the maladies found all round. The constructive work goes to the roots of wars and tries to set them right. Thus theoretically constructive work is needed to set right things everywhere. For taking any movement to the 'grass-roots' constructive work is needed.

Gandhiji discovered the various items of the constructive work whenever he found them necessary to the historical situation in which he was placed. Thus it appears that the Gandhian constructive programmes are 'context sensitive'. Gandhiji says, 'My list does not pretend to be exhaustive; it is merely illustrative'. Thus he leaves his list of constructive programmes as open and depending on the need new programmes may be added and old programmes may be interpreted and revitalised.

Chapter 1 deals with constructive work. Chapter 2 deals with constructive programme. Chapter 3 deals with Gandhian conception of man. Chapter 4 deals with Gandhiaan approach to population. Chapter 5 deals with Gandhian concept of humanism. Chapter 6 deals with individual and society. Chapter 7 deals with means and ends.

So far as the writing of this book is concerned, whatever success I have achieved is due to the relentless efforts, consistent help and encouragement of Dr. P.S.G. Kumar, Head of Library and Information Science Department of Nagpur University. I express my sincere gratitude to him.

I express my warm thanks to Prof. Dipak Joshi. Department of Fine

Arts, Nagpur University for the help and cooperation provided to me in the completion of this work. I also express my sincere thanks to Shri P.N. Hardas, Shri B.N. Nimbalkar, Shri V.C. Kori and Shri Anandrao Dhongade of Gandhian Thought Department, Nagpur University for their help in supplying a number of books to me for reference.

I will be failing in my duty if I do not thank Mr. R. Sunder, B.Com., Accountant General Office, Nagpur for his generous assistance in my endeavour.

I am also indebted to Concept Publishing Company for publishing this book in such a short span of time. Finally I hold myself to blame for the errors and shortcomings, if any. This work would have not been completed without the grace of Lord Venkateswara of Tirumala and Alamelu Thayar of Tiruchanur.

K.S. BHARATHI

CONTENTS

CONTENTS

1

CONSTRUCTIVE WORK

GANDHIJI USED the term 'construction' to express his method of rebuilding India according to his vision of a non-violent, non-exploitative social order. This method is called by him constructive work. He has not written any book on the subject. However, he has written a small pamphlet in 1941. This was latter on revised in 1945 which contain, in brief, the contents of the programme.

Meaning

'Constructive work' is a unique concept used by Gandhiji to express his method of non-violent liberation. Liberation obtained through 'Constructive work' enables everyone to enjoy freedom, equality and fraternity. There is neither winner nor looser here. Gandhiji, conceived the words 'Constructive Programme' for which 'Constructive Work' has also alternatively been used. This concept includes fabrication, structure as well as the manner of putting together the parts. Gandhiji in his early life spoke about social work. But later on, he used the words Constructive Programme instead of social work to express his special approach to rebuild man and the nation. The term 'Social Work' was replaced by 'Constructive Work' to bring out the full implication of the revolutionary approach of this non-violent method of individual and social transformation leading to Sarvodaya social order.

Constructive Programme according to Gandhiji is designed to build up the nation from the very bottom . . . it must mean complete independence in every sense of the expression. Indeed his claim that civil disobedience is not absolutely necessary to win freedom through purely non-violent effort if the cooperation of the whole nation is secured in the constructive programme. This does not mean that Constructive Work was merely a tactical instrument in a non-violent struggle against colonial regime. For Gandhiji, Constructive Work was the heart of the matter.

In 1931 Gandhiji wrote, "My work of social reform was no way less than or subordinate to political work. The fact is that when I saw that to a certain extent my social work would be impossible without the help of political work, I took to the latter and only to the extent that it helped the former. I must therefore confess that the work of social reform or self-purification of this nature is a hundred times dearer to me than what is called purely political work." The Constructive programme is therefore central to the understanding of Gandhiji's concept of Swaraj, which was for him a step towards the ultimate goal of '*Ramrajya*'.

Principles of Constructive Programme

1. It is performed of its own accord. It is purely a moral action which strengthens morality in man.
2. Cooperation and mutual aid are the importance of constructive work. Voluntariness and sharing are the core of constructive activities.
3. Self-reliance and self-help is another important principle of constructive programme.
4. The fourth principle of constructive programme is building from below.
5. Constructive programme is the concrete expression of the spirit of non-violence.
6. Decentralisation is another important principle of constructive programme.

To quote Prof. K. Arunachalamji, "In a centralised institution, one man is accountable for operational as well as managerial work. By delegation of authority and duties it is possible for the top executive to secure the willing services of several competent managers. Decentralisation promotes development of initiative, responsibility and morality among workers. When done in the proper way, it fosters personalities and improves working relationship. Four things are very necessary for the successful working of decentralisation: (1) the availability of trained, capable and devoted managers who can undertake responsibility and are willing to take decisions at their own levels, (2) an arrangement for overall supervision and guidance so that the decentralised units can be controlled by fixed and predetermined standards of performance, (3) provision of necessary service facilities which are not ordinarily available to basic units of any big organisation and (4) an animating idea that could bind the decentralised units and keep them together in spite of their autonomous functioning".

The Framework

Framework is a structure for supporting anything. Constructive Programme consists of several apparently unconnected, independent activities. But all these are united together by a framework which supports the idea of a novel revolution. Gandhiji believed in the dual revolution, in the minds of men as well as in the structure of society which brought power to local community. He was confident that his constructive programme will lead on to this happy consumation.

Gandhiji wrote in *Young India* in 1924, "I am a humble seeker after truth. I am impatient to realise myself, to attain *Moksha* in this very existence. My national service is part of my training for freeing my soul from the bondage of flesh. Thus considered, my service may be regarded as purely selfish. For me the road to salvation lies through incessant toil in the service of my country and through that of the humanity, I want to identify myself with every thing that lives. So, my patriotism is for me a state in my journey to the Land of Eternal Freedom and Peace."

Thus the framework of Constructive Programme are Truth and Non-violence supported by determination and dedication, *vairagya* and *thyaga*. Truth is the goal and non-violence is the means. The path to the goal on either side are guarded by the virtue of *vairagya* and *thyaga*.

The Content

Constructive Programme was not conceived by Gandhiji in a single day. It took several years to give shape and form to the programme. *Satyagraha* and constructive programme are closely related with each other.

In 1941 Gandhiji had listed the following thirteen items:

1. Communal Unity
2. Removal of Untouchability
3. Prohibition
4. *Khadi*

5. Other Village Industries
6. Village Sanitation
7. New or Basic Education
8. Adult Education
9. Uplift of Women
10. Education in Health and Hygiene
11. Provincial Languages
12. Propagation of *Rashtra Bhasha* and
13. Promotion of Economic Equality

In 1945 Gandhiji added the following items:

14. Kisans
15. Labour
16. Adivasis
17. Lepers
18. Students.

After Gandhiji's death the following items were added by his followers to strengthen the movement:

19. Cow Protection
20. Nature Cure
21. Bhoodan
22. Gramdan
23. Shanti Sena

The goal of Constructive work is not to provide economic relief to the unemployed or to distribute some wages to the poor but to build up a non-violent social order. In that we have not made much head way, what was needed was a superior, a more advanced type of worker, who would have a full understanding of the scientific basis of Constructive work and an awarenessly its implications in terms of non-violence. Success would depend on uttermost purity; impatience would be fatal. Gandhiji also desired that more and more workers in future be drawn from the villages themselves so that they can get under the skin of the villagers and instinctively think in terms of their thought.

Historical Development – Its Needs

Gandhiji got inspired by the play '*Harishchandra*' and decided to follow the Truth even as Harishchandra and go through ordeals consequent upon such pursuit. He was also captivated by the devotion of Shravana to his parents when he happened to read a book *'Shravana Pitribhakti Nataka'*. At the same time, he happened to see a picture of Shravana. The book and picture left such an indelible impression that he gave up even his games and play, preference to nursing his ailing father. He decided to achieve self-realisation. Subsequently Truth became his God and the means of realising the Truth was through sacrifice and service.

Gandhiji learnt in England that man's supremacy over the lower animals meant not that the former should prey upon the latter, but that the higher should protect the lower and that there should be mutual aid between the two as between man and man. This became one of the important principles in his way of life. In the history of the evolution of the concept "Constructive Work" is an important stage when the beneficiary's interest and concern is kept upper most by the benefactor. But the benefactor also moves forward in the achievement of his goal. Gandhiji says that the result of his social service was that there was not in Pretoria, no Indian I did not know, or whose conditions I was not acquainted with. This was how he identified with the joys and sufferings of the Indian community while in South Africa.

Gandhiji wanted to use his special skill for making his living and give free service to the community. He expected others also to do likewise. He says, 'Service of the poor has been my heart's desire and it has always thrown me amongst the poor and enabled me to identify myself with them'.

During the Boer War in 1899 Gandhiji collected together sufficient number of comrades and with great difficulty got their services accepted as an ambulance corps. The work of the corps was much applauded and Indian's prestige was enhanced. The leaders were awarded the war medal.

Regarding his social work in South Africa Gandhiji says, 'But I had some bitter experiences. I saw that I could not so easily count on the help of the community in getting it to do its own duty, as I could in claiming for its rights. At some places I met with insults, at others with polite indifference. It was too much for the people to better themselves to keep their surrounding clean. To expect them to find money for the work was out of question. These experiences taught me, better than ever before, that without infinite patience it was impossible to get the people to do any work. It is the reformer who is anxious for the reform, and not society from which he should expect nothing better than opposition, abhorrence and even mutual persecution why . . . the reformer holds dear as life itself'.

After returning from South Africa Gandhiji travelled from Bombay to Calcutta to participate in the Congress in 1901. He found to his sorrow the deplorable conditions of sanitation in the camp. He also saw the worst form of casteism and touch-me-notism in the shape of separate kitchen. He tried to bring home to the volunteers the secret of service. The Zulu Rebellion gave him one more opportunity to offer his unshifted services to the then Government. This work brought him into contact with many Europeans.

It was during Champaran Satyagraha that Gandhiji was convinced that work of permanent nature was impossible without proper village education. He decided to open primary schools in six villages. Besides primary education it was decided to do as much sanitary work as possible.

Gandhiji was aware of the people's partiality for exciting work and dislike for quiet constructive effort. Recollecting the incidents after Rowlatt Bill Satyagraha Gandhiji wrote, 'I realised that before a people could be fit for offering civil disobedience on a mass scale, it would be necessary to create a band of well trained pure hearted volunteers who thoroughly understand the strict conditions of *satyagraha.* They could explain these to the people and by sleepless vigilance keep them on the right path'. With this end in view he started the training of workers. But he could see that it was a difficult task to interest the people in the peaceful side of *satyagraha* and constructive work is the peaceful side of *satyagraha.*

When Gandhiji left South Africa and started his work in India, he soon realised that the great majority of Indian could not be mobilised in political work. In the year 1920 Gandhiji launched a four-fold constructive programme with spinning wheel as the main plank. During the course of freedom struggle a few more items were added. Addressing the Rajkot Workers, Gandhiji said, "All this Constructive work should be for its own sake. And be sure that this will develop the quality required for non-violent responsible government. And that is how I began my work in South Africa. I began with serving the people and I did not know that I was training them for civil disobedience. I did not know myself that I was so training myself. But you all know what happened in the end".

On 18 March, 1926 in *Young India*, Gandhiji wrote, "This

Constructive programme may go on endlessly. But why should you be tired of it? Do you know the Hundred years war in England? If they fought for a hundred years we should be prepared to fight for a thousand years, inasmuch as we are a continent. That we will have given our contribution to the fight for freedom will be our reward'. 'That is the Mass Constructive Programme I want you to do and that is the basis of the training for the non-violence of the brave. It is whole and indivisible and those who do not believe in it must leave me and work according to their own lights".

In the mid-December 1941, Gandhiji issued a 25-page booklet on 'Constructive Programme'. This was written by him in the train from Sevagram to Bardoli. He wrote in the booklet, 'If it makes no appeal to the Congressmen I must be rejected. For my handling of civil disobedience without the constructive programme will be like a paralysed hand attempting to lift a spoon'. This booklet contained thirteen items.

On 15th February, 1945 Gandhiji addressed Kasturba Nidhi workers. The booklet on Constructive work was revised with some more items added to the already existing thirteen. Gandhiji pointed out that the eighteen-fold constructive programme with the *Charkha* as its centre is the concrete expression of that spirit in an organised society.

Gandhiji pointed out that constructive work is not a strategy, or a technique of fighting. The constructive work connotes a way of life. It can be worked only by those men who have adopted it by the heart as well as by the intellect. Regarding the future direction of work he said, 'The workers of the *Charkha sangh* are not there merely to earn a living for themselves or merely to distribute some wages to the spinners, weavers, etc., by way of poor relief. The only goal worthy of their ambition must be to create a non-violent order of society'.

The concept and frame of reference of constructive work and workers have grown and taken shape in various stages from the boyhood of Gandhiji to his last days.

2

CONSTRUCTIVE PROGRAMME

Communal Unity

COMMUNAL UNITY is an important item in the constructive programme. Not only that, it is the main and basic item to prepare the mind of the people to fight for freedom and also for maintaining it after attaining the freedom.

Everyone is agreed about the necessity of communal unity – not political unity but unbreakable heart unity. Everyone should realise that he is a Hindu, Christian, Muslim, Jew, etc., at heart. He should feel his identity with every other inhabitants of India. This religious feeling along with the feeling of the removal of untouchability, equality of women, economic equality, eradication of disparity between urban and rural, agriculture and industry, equal opportunity and employment of all, hygiene and sanitation, education based on craft and vocation, etc., will surely have the way for communal unity.

Community is composed of people, rendering various essential services to the larger whole. They depend on each other. Consequently, every section of people is engaged in some productive labour which is essential to the whole community. Hence they are interdependent and useful, not only to themselves but to others also. So, everyone is a useful link in the chain of the community. If any link is useless it will become a burden and dead tissue in the link which is ruinous to the body, 'the Community'. It means, in the interest of the community, it should be removed from the body, i.e., Community. That is to say, the idle and unproductive section of the community is a dead weight and it should be removed from the community, otherwise, it will spoil the whole community by resorting to unsocial trickeries and exploitations. The pillars of the supporters of the community that is the producers whether they produce food, cloth, oil, pot, baskets, mats, etc., or who shave our hairs, wash our clothes, clean our streets, latrines, etc., they are doing good to the community by bestowing their labour and skill.

They should be honoured. But those who are doing no productive labour to the community, is a thief, a sinner, an exploiter, a waste and dead weight to the community. So, such people should be removed from the community.

Today, the structure of society is in a reverse position wherein people who do not produce anything for himself or others are held in high esteem and the people who are doing the most essential labour are treated with utmost contempt. The lesser the work greater the honour. More and more the useful labour less and less respect and at the end, more and more degradation. This is the present position of the social structure.

Dr. Rajendra Prasad had given the following illustrations of occasions on which trouble ordinarily arises and how non-violence may be effectively employed:

1. A Muslim wants to sacrifice a cow or slaughter it for food. A Hindu will try to dissuade him from carrying out his wish by friendly argument and by appealing to him not to offend Hindu sentiments. In no circumstances will he or a group of Hindus resort to violence to prevent the act.
2. Similarly, if a Hindu takes out the image of Durga in procession before a Mosque and the Muslim is even disturbed during his prayer time by the music, the latter may not use force but will try his level best to dissuade the Hindu by entreaty.
3. If either a Muslim or a Hindu wishes to build a Mosque or dedicate a temple to an image on his own land, either should recognise the right of the other.
4. If the *aazan* of the Muslim or the *aarati* of the Hindu disturbs either party, the temporary inconvenience must be borne with due regard to each other's feelings.
5. To preach and propagate one's religion is the right of everyone. But in exercising the right the utmost care must be taken not to hurt 'the feelings of those belonging to other faiths by decrying their creeds or their founders or revered saints'.
6. Conversion of a person from one faith to another is common source of rousing bitter feelings of revenge. This should not be.
7. In the matter of kidnapping the members of the offending community should consider it a point of honour with them to bring the guilty to book.
8. Other illustrations may be given of occasions which lead to

violence between the parties concerned. Violence should be eschewed under all circumstances. If friendly persuasion fails, resort can always be had to arbitration by an impartial person or persons acceptable to both parties. If one party refuses to have arbitration, the non-violent method of protest through self-suffering may be used in order to meet the opponent's heart, provided it is a clear case and the person concerned is strong enough to resist the evil in this way. If a non-violent protest is impossible, justice may even be sought in law courts or from other constituted authority. What applies to Hindus and Muslims applies equally to all communities.

9. Of late much bad blood seems to be caused by what are said to be attacks on the culture of a particular community by another. This may not cause riots, but it is no less serious for it spreads the poison in an insidious manner. Then, too, there is such a thing as an insidious force which a majority may use constantly against a minority. Conversely a minority may exercise disproportionate power on account of its wealth, physical strength or even because of the cowardice of others. In all these cases it should be the constant endeavour of all to try to set at rest the doubts and suspicious of others by their own lives and prove from their day-to-day activity that no harm is intended and that all are free to live and think as they like. Thus, for example, there should be perfect freedom for everyone regarding language, regarding the education of children and the ordering of their lives.
10. In the matter of trades and professions there should not be unhealthy rivalry or jealousy. No trade or profession may be said to be the exclusive right of anyone community. Everyone should be free to carry on the trade or profession he likes. If in any big concern, shop or factory the owner employs members of his own community, it should not be made a bone of contention.
11. Political power perhaps furnishes the most subtle and devastating causes for mutual distrust and suspicion. Every community should cast out once and for all the desire or ambition to rule over others. India has so many communities that it is impossible to have peace and prosperity if any one of them tries to establish its supremacy. It should be the duty of members of one community to seek and utilise every opportunity of doing a good turn to members of other communities. Generosity and justice need not be contradictory terms. Generosity is, in fact, a potent force in

removing mistrust and ill-will. Cowardice and fear should have no place in our dealings. It is for political parties to devise ways and means of a political nature for bridging the present gulf, but individual workers can make an enormous contribution by setting an example to tolerance and patience in the face of the utmost provocation. It should be within the bounds of possibility for everyone to cultivate intimate friendship with at least one member of the other community. It is such small seeds well sown that will grow into fruitful trees. One golden rule to be scrupulously observed is not to judge others. It is always best to turn the searchlight inwards and lay one's finger on one's own weakness and shortcomings. It follows, therefore, that in times of communal strife members of each community should try to set right their own thoughts and actions and those of their own community and leave the other community to its own members. Statements hastily issued to the press, inaccuracy in facts, imputation of motives, and retaliation create bad blood and make reconciliation difficult. Truth must be brought to light, but statements and counter-statements often aggravate rather than mitigate ill-will.

12. The organisation of bands of men and women imbued with the spirit of non-violence and willing to lay down their lives, if necessary, is most desirable both from the point of view of preventing and of controlling communal riots. Every volunteer of such a *shantidal* must undergo a period of training. The task is a difficult one and requires courage and faith of the highest order. Fitness for such work can best come from long apprenticeship in the service of all communities. Whenever and wherever possible, members of one community should make it a point of living among and serving members of other communities. This would open the way to intimate social contacts and create mutual understanding. Indeed such workers will not only be able to prevent riots but will also be able to stop their spread for they will be beloved of the people.
13. A standing committee of members of all communities for every town and group of villages commanding the confidence of the people would be of great help and might well serve as a board of arbitration in cases of dispute.

Gandhiji had devoted much of his time in maintaining peace in the latter part of his life in the Indian Society which was torn by communal strife.

India is a land of people with different religious faiths and diverse customs and habits. But sporadic clashes between the Hindus and Muslims who use to live as brethren were witnessed. The main causes for the conflicts among them were the slaughter of cows by the Muslims and the music accompanying Hindu processions in front of mosques. The communal conflicts were fostered by the British Government which encouraged divisive forces by introducing communal electorates and fanning the fire of communal consciousness.

Gandhiji realised the importance of Hindu-Muslim unity from the earliest period of his public career in India. So he had the Hindu-Muslim or Communal Unity as the first item in his Constructive Programme. His writings and his speeches of those days were a passionate plea for communal harmony and unity.

The conflicts between the Hindus and Muslims were deepened when the Muslim League demanded a separate, independent State for the Muslims. Gandhiji knew that separating the people by arousing religious sentiments and making them feel that they were enemies would result only in bloodshed. When India got Independence, the new State of Pakistan was formed. He wanted to attain freedom through non-violence and unity. But freedom came to India with disunity and hatred. In many places of the northern provinces, the conditions worsened as the murder of the Hindus by the Muslims, and of the Muslims, by the Hindus was increasing in number and the cruelties inflicted by one community on another and the consequent retaliation became regular features. Gandhiji decided to check the mob violence even at the cost of his violence. He walked barefoot on a pilgrimage of penance through villages where the communal riots were going on. When he had withstood the angry crowds in Calcutta and wandered alone through the villages of Bengal, Lord Mountbatten called him the 'One-man boundary force'. It is worth remembering at this juncture that Gandhiji gave his life only for the sake of maintaining communal peace among the Hindus and the Muslims.

Removal of Untouchability

According to *Biblical* and *Rig Vedic* stories, God created a man and a woman. We are all descendants of those two. Then, where is the possibility for various ancestors to produce various castes and untouchability? Once our ancesters were cave-dwellers who ate the flesh of animals which they hunted. Then, they lived nomadic life, tending cattles, roaming round the pastoral lands.

History

According to Indian history, the Arya Brahmins were noted for beef-eating until yesterday i.e., until the dawn of Buddhism. They were not originally vegetarians. The Brahmins who call themselves to be the custodian of Hindu religion and cows, were the first to accept services under the beef-eating Britishers. Even now, they give utmost respect to the beef-eating white people and enjoy the service under them more than anybody else. If they really hate beef-eating they would have treated the beef-eating whites as contemptuously as they treat the untouchables. Conversions to Islam took place by people almost from all castes in India.

Therefore, we cannot say which caste came from what caste and what was the past status of the present castes including the untouchables. Lot of changes have taken place beyond recognition. In Kerala and Tamil Nadu, within the span of eight years, castes which were considered to be low or untouchables have come to a highly esteemed status now. Therefore, nobody should be under the impression that the so-called present low castes or untouchables were held at the lower rank in the past too.

The Crime of Untouchability

Gandhiji is of the opinion that it is a crime committed by the so-called high caste Hindus. He says, 'To remove untouchability is a penance that caste Hindus owe to Hinduism and to themselves. We have degraded them and then have the audocity to use their very degradation against their use'. Again he painfully says, 'That religion and that nation will be blotted out of the face of the earth which pins its faith to injustice, untruth and violence. God is light, not darkness, God is love, not hate, God is truth, not untruth'.

Gandhiji is of the opinion that there will be no *swaraj* along with untouchability. He says that unless this condition is fulfilled we will gain *swaraj* only to lose it the next moment. About Hinduism, he says, 'If I found that Hinduism really counteranced untouchability, I should have no hesitation in renouncing Hinduism itself'. In Hinduism there is no sanction for treating a single human being as untouchable.

Dr. B.R. Ambedkar is of the opinion that Hinduism is the root cause for this evil of caste and untouchability and therefore Hinduism should be eradicated root and branch to do away with these two evils, namely caste and untouchability. So long as Hinduism lives, caste will also exist. So long as caste exists, untouchability too will exist. Therefore, if we want to put an end to untouchability, the caste should be annihilated. If caste is to go, Hindu religion should be uprooted and destroyed.

Untouchability and Economics

The stratification of society – from Brahmin at the top to the untouchable at the bottom – is a clever judicious arrangement to shift the burden of labour on the shoulders of the lower by the higher castes. Without doing any labour one should earn more and live happily, commanding more influence. This is the hallmark of the higher caste. The untouchables are prohibited from carrying on certain avocations, on the ground of birth according to *Varnashrama Dharma* as well as in actual practice. Even if he is allowed to do certain jobs, the untouchable fellow will be paid less wage than that of his high caste counterpart. In short, however much they are efficient or industrious, the Harijans cannot run a hotel, a shop, a business etc. They should not compete; they won't be tolerated by the high caste men. They are considered to be slaves who are assigned hard manual productible labour.

To obtain equality, raising the economic status is indispensable. Economic equality is a major factor to wipe out other discrimination and to bring about equality in other spheres. The foundation of economy, especially in India, rests on land. The untouchables are all sturdy labourers. Hence they are made to be slaves under selfish high caste people who are interesting them. Secondly, the untouchables should be given proper training, capital, tools and machines to start various industries along with credit facilities through co-operatives and nationalised banks. Thus, economic equality will go a long way to solve the problem of untouchability and bring about social equality.

Untouchability and Education

The progress of any community of nation depends on the nature of education imparted. It is through the forces of education, both formal and informal, that human standards and ideals are raised. Educational development, therefore is the essential prerequisite to the all round development of any community. The Brahmins command their respect mainly because of their education. Therefore, if the untouchables are to be lifted and made to realise their own strength and importances and to stand on their own legs, proper education should be imparted to them.

Inter-Dining and Inter-Marriage

To quote Gandhiji, 'Restraint upon inter-dining is no part of *Varna Dharma*, but I do not understand why inter-dining retards the evolution of the soul. In other words untouchability cannot constitute any ground for restraint on inter-dining or inter-marriage'. To get rid of the castes and untouchability, the surest and durable method is inter-marriage. Sexual intercourse between man and woman of different castes and that of between the caste-Hindu and Harijans are common. If equal opportunities are given in all spheres to Harijans in par with the caste Hindus, and inter-marriage between the Harijans and the caste-Hindus, is legalised, inter-marriage will become common and, thereby, the caste barriers will disappear and consequently untouchability will also come to an end. Now-a-days inter-dining is slowly gaining ground. It is not a serious problem when compared with education, economic, religious and other problems facing Harijans.

Separate Electorate for the Harijans

Gandhiji said that 'the question of separate electorates for the untouchables is a modern manufacture of a Satanic Government. The only thing needed is put them on the voters list and provide for fundamental right for them in the constitution. Separate electorates to the untouchables will ensure them bondage in perpetuity. The Musalmans will never cease to be Musalmans by having separate electorates. Do you want the untouchables to remain untouchables for ever? Well, the separate orthodox Hindu would have to approach them for votes'.

Dr. B.R. Ambedkar is of the opinion that in a 'Joint electorates', the representative of the untouchable is not a true representative of the depressed class people. He is not their spokesman. He is only an 'yes man', 'a hand lifter' to the high caste people by whose majority votes he is elected. He is neither chosen by the depressed class people nor elected by their votes, their votes being minority. In this system, the untouchable who is a slave to the high caste people, who is a coward, fearing to express the feelings and interest of the depressed people, who is a mouth piece of the high caste majority alone can bag the votes of the high caste people who are the majority voters who decide the victory can win the election. The true representative of the depressed class people will stand to lose even though he gets the entire number of the depressed class votes. Under this circumstances, in the system of joint electorates, no depressed class representative can win in the election and represent the cause of his community in the assembly or in the Parliament. Hence separate electorates is the only alternative to give a chance to the depressed class people to represent their case.

According to separate electorates system, a depressed class man is chosen from among them. Every depressed class man has two votes, one to cast for the depressed class candidates, another for high caste Hindu candidates. For the success of the depressed class candidates, depressed class votes alone are taken into account. The depressed class candidates who gets the majority of the depressed class votes, will succeed, and not the candidate also who gets more votes of the high class Hindu people. Therefore in this system the depressed class man who is really representing the depressed people alone can become the member of an Assembly or the Parliament, and not the man who is overwhelmingly supported by the high caste-Hindu voters. Consequently, in this system a depressed class candidate need not cringe the high caste people or he need not give up his ideology or policy against the interest of the depressed class people in favour of the high caste-Hindus. Another advantage of this system is that the high caste-Hindus will always come to the depressed class man for vote. That is the high caste people will depend on the depressed class man for getting his vote; whereas the depressed class man will completely independent of the high caste-Hindus in this regard.

Untouchables and Reservation

Gandhiji is not against reservation of posts, appointments; and positions to be allotted to the depressed class people. Dr. B.R. Ambedkar fought for reservation. He told that the reason for his fight for the reservation of posts in the Government services and in the legislature and the judiciary, is that the untouchables were ill-treated and humiliated by others because there was no depressed class people in those posts. He pleaded that untouchables should be given as many posts as to the ratio of their population. He condemned giving more than 90 per cent of the seats to the people who constitute 3 per cent of the population. Even today what Dr. Ambedkar said is true.

Now-a-days, a new argument is in the air. That is, instead of social base, only economic base should be taken into account for giving aid or scholarship for education or for giving jobs. Another new argument in the air is efficiency or merit. It means those who get the highest mark in the examination or the test held will be given the job.

According to Mandal Commission until the caste is abolished and untouchability eradicated and equality established, there should be reservation in proportion to the socially and educationally backwardness, or at least in proportion to the respective caste population.

Untouchability and Conversion

According to Gandhi, conversion is not a remedy. To get rid of the stigma attached to the untouchables, one remedy suggested to untouchables is rejection of Hinduism and wholesale conversion to Islam or Christianity. If the inhuman treatment of the *Panchamas* were a part of Hinduism, its rejection would be a paramount duty both for them and those like me who would not make a fetish even of religion and condone every evil in its sacred name. But I believe that untouchability is no part of Hinduism. It is rather its excrescence to be removed by every effort.

But we may not grumble if Harijans change their faith in order to better their material conditions and to secure protection from persecution. In converting oneself to Christianity one cannot get rid of the stigma attached to his caste. But if a depressed classman converts himself to Islam, he is able to get rid of the social disabilities undergone by him previously, and is easily able to move freely with others, whose recognition he can easily perceive. If conversion is allowed for material and mundane facts, why cannot the conversion based on spirituality also be permitted, as God exists in every religion. Therefore, if other things failed, conversion to Islam seems to be a wayout for solving the problem. But generally it is better to get rid of this problem without changing the religion.

Untouchability and Government

Government is composed of peoples. Untouchables constitute more than 20 per cent of the population. Hence the untouchables are the part and parcel of the democratic Government. Consequently Government has its bounden duty to the untouchables even though it cannot impose a reform which its people cannot assimilate. A wise Government welcomes and needs to support and warmth and encouragement of such an agitation in order to achieve a reform which the government itself wants and I have no shadow of a doubt that if the Hindus could with one voice expressed their wish, monster of untouchability would go. It could be wrong therefore, to ascribe our own lethargy, slothfulness to the Government. The present Government, being the peoples Government, removal of untouchability is one of its duty, said Gandhiji.

Untouchability and Law

Untouchability will not be removed by the force, even of law. It can only be removed when the majority of Hindus realise that it is crime against God and man, and are ashamed of it. In other words, it is a process of conversion, that is purification of the Hindu heart. The aid of law has to be invoked when it hinders or interferes with the progress of the reform as when in spite of the willingness of the Trustees and the Temple going public law prohibits the opening of a particular temple. In democracy, law is the expression of the peoples willingness. If once law is passed, it means the willingness is expressed openly, and, therefore, it should be executed somehow or other severely until the goal is achieved. For any social reform like the removal of untouchability, it needs attack on two sides, one from the people through change of heart, another from Government through the force of law. Both are necessary.

Prohibition

Alcohol: An Historical Survey

Alcoholic drinks made from fermented food-stuffs have been in use from ancient times. Fermented drinks were known to the ancient Assyrians, Chinese, Greeks, etc.

The law giver of Babylon provided as early as 2250 B.C. death penalty to the wine-seller. The spartan law also imposed the same penalty on warriors who were found to be drunkards. The Carthaginians imposed rigorous restrictions on soldiers drinking while on active service.

Pythagoras considered drunkenness to be identical with ruin. Xenophon said, "Temperance means first moderation in healthiful indulgence and secondly abstinence from things dangerous, such as the use of intoxicating wines".

Four thousand years ago, a Chinese emperor forbade the use of intoxicants and, as a divine consequence, it is believed that heavens raised gold for three days upon the people. Chan dynasty and Yuan dynasty were up against drinking, manufacture and sale.

Drinks were known in India in Vedic and post-Vedic times. But intoxicating drink was severely objected in *Puranas, Shastras* and *Śmritis*. There are several references in the *Manu Smriti* condemning drinking and laying down severe punishments and penances for drinkers. Kautilya in his *Arthasasthra* devoted a whole chapter to the regulation of liquor traffic in the land, giving elaborate injunctions.

Buddhism also denounced drinking. In Islam there is a very strong taboo against beverage alcohol. It was said that during the fight from Mecca, the Prophet and his followers fought with various tribes. One battle was lost because some of them had been gambling and drinking and were unable to discharge their duties.

Emperor Akbar prohibited the sale of drinks and permitted only Christians to drink. Lord Hastings when he came to India, observed, 'The simplicity of the living and the conduct of Indians, can clearly be seen from their simple food and their complete abstinence from intoxicants'.

Alcohol and Health

The alcohol has been defined from the physiological and medical view point as 'an intoxicating, hypnotic, analgesic, anaesthetic, narcotic, poisonous and potentially habit-forming or addictive drug or chemical'. It can be produced by fermentation of any substance containing sugar. Alcohol is a narcotic which means that it causes stupefaction. It is anaesthetic in the sense that it puts the brain to sleep.

To quote Dr. Emil Bogen, 'Alcohol is an important and widely used poison. . . . No other poison causes so many deaths or leads to or intensifies so many diseases both physical and mental as does alcohol in the various forms in which it is taken. No text-book on Nutrition treats alcohol as a food. Instead medical books classify it under drugs and poisons. It has been scientifically established'.

Alcohol slows down the function of the body whether it is the beating of the heart, the thinking process or the attack of white corpuscles upon sources of infection. It mixes readily with all blood fluids. Drink deprives him of all scruples and noble impulses. He is in the grip of violent emotion.

A distinguished physicians of England, Sir Victor Horsley named the following diseases in which alcohol was a direct causative factor: 1. acute alcoholic poisoning; 2. acute mania; 3. Delirium tremens; 4. chronic alcoholic insanity; 5. alcoholic epilepsy; 6. alcoholic neuritis and 7. alcoholic paralysis. He listed the following diseases in which alcohol is frequently a determining or a contributing cause: 1. Pharyngitis; 2. gastric catarrh; 3. congestion of liver; 4. cirrhosis of liver; 5. fatty liver; 6. albuminuria; 7. brights diseases; 8. gout; 9. glycosuira; 10. inflammation of the skin; 11. functional disorders; 12. dilation of heart; 13. fatty heart; 14. arterio sclerosis; 15. consumption; 16. increased susceptibility to the inflammation of the lungs; 17. chronic dyspepsia; 18. dilation of the stomachs; 19. bronchial catarrh; 20. epilepsy; 21. melancholia; 22. hysteria; 23. desalination; 24. lidiocy; 25. sun stroke; 26. erysipelas; 27. blood poisoning; 28. tubercle; 29. syphilis; 30. diphtheria; 31. cholera and 32. increased susceptibility to the inflammatory diseases of the eyes and 33. lead poisoning.

Alcohol has little place in modern scientific medicine as a therapeutic agent. Dr. Howord Kelly observed, 'There is no single disease in the world of which alcohol is the cure'.

Alcohol and Crime

More crimes are committed by persons when under the influence of alcohol than when they are sober. In crimes against persons, 51 per cent were attributed to liquor. It is found that partial or complete intoxication is an important element in many types of crimes and charges of criminality. These include arson, attempted burglary, sex offence, shooting, stabbing, robbery, man slaughter, defrauding an inn-keeper, carrying concealed weapons, assault and violation of the out-law.

To quote Frederick Burnest, 'Four of the major police problems from time immemorial have been immorality, gambling, narcotics, and liquor'. Crime increases or decreases according to the account of alcohol consumed.

There is a close relationship between alcohol and the social problem of crime. The State which lifted the Prohibition Act cannot escape its responsibility in provoking lawlessness and in bringing about all the liquor causal evils. Its contributions to evils, immoralities, crimes of violence and carnage on the road cannot be mitigated by the special plea of sharing a part of the ill-rotten gains of the liquor business.

Alcohol and Machine Age

When a drinking man is handling a machine, whether mounted on wheels or imbedded in the ground, he incurs a tremendous risk, and become a source of danger not only to himself but to many others working close by who may not have had anything to do with drinking. The modern machine insists on single minded attention and careful and accurate handling.

Alcohol assumes responsibility for accidents both directly or indirectly. Forty per cent of traffic accidents are due to alcohol. Safe handling of machines requires clear vision, good hearing, accurate judgement and quick reaction. All these functions are adversely affected by alcohol.

Alcohol and Industry

A drinking workman does not put in his quota of working hours and is inefficient. A drinking workman's turnover is poor; attendance irregular; and while working, his judgement, accuracy and endurance suffer. Marshal. B. Clinard observed that the Problem drinkers had 2.9 times as many days absence, 2.5 as many cases of illness of injury-cause, and absence of 8 days or more than the others. The cost of sickness payment was 3.2 times as great and in the case of women drinkers problem twice as much. According to the Census Bureau the reduced liquor consumption lowered the death rate also. It also estimated that the pauperism ratio become the lowest in the history of the country.

The late Sri. M.S. Mannamwar gives a glowing picture on the

effect of prohibition. He says, 'prior to its introduction these industrial estates, be they in big cities or in mofussils, were always an open exhibition of poverty, dirt, misery, unruly domestic and group quarrels. Not a single night would pass without a major anti-social event, the root cause of which was excessive indulgence in alcohol drinks. The pay pockets reaching home, if they reached at all, were small and there was complete neglect of family and children. Schooling children were utterly neglected and the colonies were full of irresponsible vagabonds urchins. I have seen with my own eyes a complete transformation taking place in these very industrial estates with the same inhabitants after the introduction of prohibition. Today in these industrial estates there is a much greater degree of peace and harmony and the social life of the families is very much normal. The estates are clean and the residents take pride in the fact their children are coming up as good citizen. I would, therefore, conclude that prohibition has definitely done a large volume of good to the low paid working class population and their families and if anything it has helped them in raising their standard of living'.

The Economics of Alcohol

Liquor and poverty are close companions. Liquor has found at all times and in all claims, an enemy of affluence. Among the low income group it plays havoc, blasting their lives, reducing them to perpetual penury and making the dependents destitutes. It will not be an exaggeration to say that drink has been one of the principal causes of poverty and it has impoverished individual families, class and the community. Of all the evil effects of drink its assault on the poor people was felt by Gandhiji, the most. While in South Africa he remarked, 'one of the most greatly felt evils of the British rule is the importation of alcohol, that enemy of mankind, that curse of civilisation in some form or another'. Again he said, 'The Government it seems instead of stopping are aiding and abetting the spread of alcohol. The poor there as everywhere are the greatest sufferers. It is they who spend what little they earn in buying alcohol instead of buying good food and other necessaries. It is that wretched poor man who has to starve his family, who has to break the sacred trust of looking after his children, if any, in order to drink himself into misery and premature deaths. There is no more potent instrument of evil than drunkenness'.

The money that a workman pays for his drink is generally more than the cost of good meal for him and often quite enough for a good meal for the whole family. To quote C. Rajagopalachari, 'The most urgent reason for prohibition is the good of these depressed classes. No other single measure of reform can help these people, and at once raise them economically and socially as total prohibition can. The rich and the educated may be indifferent about the reform. It is most necessary for saving the poor and the lowly'.

Alcohol and Society

To Gandhiji total prohibition was tantamount to moral elevation. Instead of being a blessing physically, intellectually and economically, drink sapped both body and soul. He felt that liquor shops were an insufferable curse imposed upon society, and liquor traffic could be brought under effective control only by prohibition. The nation responded to his clarion call against drink, and as a result of national upsurge against insoberity effective steps were taken in the pre-independents and post-independence decade, to give prohibition a place of honour.

Alcohol and Education

Education is a must to save the society from the drink evil. Enlightened education will lead to better law enforcement and a strong public opinion will keep the indifferent and apathetic administration. It has to be a nation-wide effort, the corner-stone of which is a nation-wide programme of education. People must be educated through books, pamphlets, films, radio, audio-visual materials, film stripes, slides, etc.

The concept of education has a wider base than mere banishment of ignorance. According to Tryon Edwards, 'the greatest end of education is to discipline rather than to furnish the mind'. Toynbee has said that alcoholism has been the cause of decay of 19 out of 21 civilisations as also the cause of athesism, materialism and racialism. This is certainly true of the fall of Babylonian, Greek and Roman civilisations.

The following facts regarding the effect of drink should be proclaimed:

1. It increases traffic casualties, both fatal and non-fatal.
2. It produces several million alcoholies who ultimately become

brainless breathing corpses.

3. It produces economic waste, and leads to want and destitution.
4. It leads to human debasement and moral degeneration.
5. It breeds crimes, delinquency, disorderly behaviour and lawlessness.
6. It undermines security of the state and weakens its defence.

Dr. Ivy suggested a six-point educational programme:

1. Education should be directed towards developing public opinion to facilitate the enforcement officers to enforce the law related to alcohol in accordance with their spirit.
2. There should be an education programme which will create public support for education in junior and senior schools regarding the effects of alcoholic beverage.
3. Increasing number of recreational facilities for the youth must be provided everywhere.
4. A proper mental hygiene should be provided in the educational institutions for developing right attitude and ideas with an emphasis on religious background.
5. A successful alcohol education should be directed to unpopularise liquor and to make drinking unfashionable.
6. Every youngman should be enabled to know certain deadly effects of alcohol which are inconvertible and inescapable.

Alcohol and Polities

The present day politicians are not concerned with principles or even with policies; he is interested only in power and prerequisites. The present day politician serves himself first, his party later and his country last, that is never in India because here caste interest dominates nation's interest.

According to Gladstone, 'The proper function of a Government is to make it easy for the people to do good and difficult for them to do evil. The excise policy of the states is facilitating the people to do evil and is making it hard for them to do good. A policy based on multiplication of taverns and increased production of intoxicating drink is a travesty of Indian tradition, a mockery of Indian culture, a caricature of Indian civilisation and a slavish subservience to Bacchanalism profligacy'.

In 1956 the Parliament had passed an unanimous resolution supporting prohibition. We cannot expect politicians to do anything in favour of prohibition. We must educate people, organise and create people's power in favour of prohibition as done by Gandhiji. As Edmund Burk said that if bad people combines, the good must associate. If we remain mere onlookers without doing anything, especially when the governments have deserted the people and defeated to their enemy, the vice will be breed, when virtue will become a weed and thereby, we will face our end.

Thus, by creating people's power, we can successfully make the country dry by bringing prohibition law and enforce it effectively with the help of education and legislation.

Khadi

The moment for the revival of hand-spinning and hand-weaving and other subsidiary processes is based on two fundamental facts of Indian life. Eighty per cent of India's population is either engaged in or dependent on agriculture, but in as much as agriculture does not occupy the entire time of the agriculturist, he has plenty of leisure to spare which might well be devoted to a supplementary occupation. Spinning and weaving not only supply this need, not only solve the problem of clothing the villager but also make a substantial addition to his slender resources. It has never been suggested that those who earn more in any other occupation should give up their work and take to spinning. It is pre-eminently a supplementary industry.

Khadi may be produced for sale as also for use by the producer himself. The khadi produced for sale is for those who do not spin themselves. Efforts have been made to improve the tools of production in order to produce better and finer yarn. The results are astonishing. The improvement in the texture of khadi, to say nothing of the variety now available, as compared with the first efforts of 22 years ago is there for all to see. The most fastidious tastes can be satisfied. But khadi cannot, indeed it is not meant to, compete with mill cloth. It should be purchased and used to the exclusion of all other cloth regardless of its higher cost by those who love the villager and stand for India's freedom. The All India Spinner Association has opened several production and sale centres, and each worker has to become a self-appointed agent for all such. He should study the economics and ethics of khadi thoroughly so that he may be able effectually to carry its message of salvation and uplift to every home. By creating a love of and demand for khadi in his locality he will lessen the difficulty experienced by many warehouses of accumulated stocks and consequent locking up of capital.

One warning is necessary in the sphere of sales. The main object of the movement is to help the poorest and humblest among us and enable them to earn an honest living through an honourable occupation. It follows that genuine khadi is only that which subserves and fulfils this purpose. In spite of the AISA's resolve to give certificates only to those individuals or institutions that sell khadi after giving the minimum wage to the extreme poverty of the spinners and weavers and by paying them a pittance sell handwoven and hand-spun at cheaper rates. It is the workers' duty to warn everyone against buying such uncertified khadi.

But while khadi production for sale must continue to be properly organised, hand-spun and hand-woven can become universal only if its utility in national economy is brought home to the people at large and they take to spinning. A spinner with average skill can spin about 400 yards in an hour which means 12,000 yards a month if he spins an hour a day. Of course the fineness of the yarn depends on the quality of the slivers and the skill of the spinner. But if we take the average count to be 10 to 12, 12,000 yards of yarn will yield about four square yards of khadi. A person can, therefore, spin enough yarn to give himself 48 square yards of cloth in a year with only an hour's spinning a day. The average consumption of cloth in our country is not more than 16 yards per head. An average spinner can thus produce enough cloth for three persons. It is perfectly easy for the agriculturist as well as those engaged in the so-called liberal professions to spare an hour every day for spinning. The national gain will be enormous. In a family of five, if two persons spin regularly for one hour every day, they can clothe the entire family.

Every worker should spin enough for his own requirements. He should be an efficient spinner on the *charkha*, the *dhanush takli* and the *takli*. He should have a thorough knowledge of all the processes prior to spinning-picking, cleaning, ginning, carding, slivering and spinning. He should know how to ment the wheel and the *dhanush takli* if anything goes wrong with them. All his tools should always be clean and in good order. By his aptness, keenness, intimate knowledge of his work, and personal example he will be able to draw people to khadi as no amount of propaganda and argument can. He should have knowledge of the art of weaving also. He may leave the work of spinning for wages to be organised by the AISA. His main work should be to organise spinning from the point of view of self-sufficiency. No capital is required for this purpose. All that is required in the worker in addition to the above qualifications is skill in imparting his knowledge to others. Each worker may take a plan according to his circumstances and the conditions of his locality. If he were to resolve to make 12 persons self-sufficient in khadi in six months and as efficient and keen spinners as himself, he will have done a great deal towards inducing others to take to it. There is hardly a village where cotton is not grown or where it cannot be had on payment. As a matter of fact every agriculturist should be persuaded to grow enough cotton to serve his personal requirements. There is again hardly a locality where there are no weavers perishing for want of employment. All this soil is ready for the worker to till and cultivate. Faith, zeal, intelligence and efficiency in the art of khadi-making alone are required for revolutionising the entire face of village life.

Village Industries

Village industry par excellence is obviously agriculture, for it provides us with all the articles of food as also the raw material for clothing. But here industry has a technical meaning. The better word, perhaps, is handicrafts. It is the decay of handicrafts in our villages that has been the cause of their ruin and made agriculture itself uninteresting and even unprofitable. For the agriculturist is idle for practically, if not more than, half the year.

All grain is produced in the field. Wheat and other grains have to be ground into flour, paddy has to be husked and made into rice, pulses have to be broken and the husk removed from the kernel. All these processes used in the old days to be performed in the village homes, but now rice, flour and *dal* mills have largely displaced the *dhenki* and *chakki* and have not only caused unemployment but have also reduced the vitamin value of food to the detriment of our bodily health. The same applies to oil seeds. Oil being an essential element of diet we may not allow it to be deprived of its vitamins. Sugar is an important item in our daily food. Sugarcane is easily grown, and from time immemorial the village *kolhus* have provided the sugar requirements of the people. But now mills have stepped in here too. Another method of getting sugar in an easily assimilable form is honey from bees. The latter can be reared without much difficulty or labour. Vegetables and fruits are important items of diet and can and should be grown in villages. Last, though by no means least, there is milk and its products which necessitate knowledge of dairying and care and scientific breeding of cattle. Special attention has therefore to be paid to:

1. Improved methods of agriculture for producing grain, cotton, sugarcane.
2. Revival of the *dhenki* and *chakki* for husking paddy, grinding wheat and breaking pulses.
3. Revival of oil *ghanis* for extracting oil from oilseeds.
4. Revival of *kolhus* for making *gur* out of sugarcane
5. Development of the science of bee-keeping.
6. Scientific methods of dairying and breeding of cattle.
7. Vegetable and fruit culture.
8. The general turning of waste into wealth as in the matter of good manure, for which intelligent use of human and animal excreta, vegetable and fruit peel, leaving of food, leaves, ashes, bones, and flesh of dead animals, etc., is of enormous value.
9. The improvements of all tools and implements for agricultural purposes and their production and manufacture in the villages themselves.

After food and clothing comes shelter. Sometimes, for social reasons, even more importance is attached to dwelling houses than to food and clothing. It is important from the point of view of village economy to see that as far as possible our houses are made with materials found in the village and by the employment of village labour. There is an economy in nature which the modern age seems to overlook. Geologists say that it takes millions of years to produce a layer of coal, mineral oil, iron ore or any other metal or mine product. We use coal, metals and mineral oils lavishly without any thought of replacing what we consume. Nature invariably observes this economy but we interfere with nature, in a sense, and in the pride of our scientific knowledge, we think that nothing of exhausting nature's store. Far-sighted people have already begun to speculate as to the time in which the world's store of oil, coal and metals will be exhausted if we continue to use them as extravagantly as we do today. But that is a problem primarily for the machine-driven countries to face. Our village economy depends on replacing what we spend. Take the fuel used in villages, for example. We use stalks of a pulse such as *arhar* and wood, and our stock can never fail. In house building, therefore, we should also use such materials as is easily replaceable. Bricks and tiles can be baked without coal, and rafters and doors can be made out of our endless store of timber. A minimum of metal need be used, and comfortable dwelling houses can be constructed without much cost. We should remember that the most wonderful and durable architecture that we have in the world was built with such materials before coal, cement and steel came into use.

Apart from these absolutely essential articles of daily use there are scores of others that man needs today with more or less urgency. These range from a needle or pin to a motor-car, a railway train or ship, from pen to ink to a printing press, from an earthern wick to electricity and so on. We have to choose wisely from among our requirements and see what can be best and easily manufactured in villages. It will be found that there are hundreds of articles which village artisans can easily produce. There are places where raw material is easily available, where tradition still persists of making particular things, and where climatic and other considerations make them indispensable. We have to seek out and encourage all such handicrafts. Take paper-making, for example, or leather articles. Raw material and workers are available for both these industries in every village. What is needed is alertness and circumspection and above all the conviction that in a country like ours with its vast resources and immense population, largely unemployed, there must and can be found employment for all. Large-scale industry may be necessary for certain of our requirements, but our village life, our culture and art have languished because our cottage industries have died to a large extent. These must be revived, if village India has to be resuscitated. Therefore as Gandhiji has so poetically described it let khadi be the sun round which all the lesser planets will revolve, and let all who wish to serve the villages use as far as possible nothing but village products.

Village Sanitation

Village sanitation is concerned with the body and environment. The village sanitation is not sanitation at all. It is insanitation. It is so abhorrible that the approach to many villages is not refreshing experience. In this respect we should, even today, accept what was told by Miss Mego. Often one would like to shut one's eyes and staff one's nose; such is the surrounding dirt and offending smell. A sense of national or social sanitation is not a virtue among us. We may take a kind of bath, but we do not mind dirtying the well or the tank or the river by whose side or in which we perform ablutions.

A review of any recorded data strikingly portrays the preventable mortality and morbidity our population is suffering from. These diseases are caused by the pollution of air, water and food by micro-organisms and insects and other, vectors of diseases. Diseases such as hook-worms, guinea-worms, filariasis, etc., which are responsible for a considerable amount of morbidity in the population, are to a large extent due to inadequacy or lack of environmental hygienic conditions.

While considering the problem of environmental hygiene with particular reference to rural areas one has to bear in mind to the totality of factors in operation — the capability and ability for the provision and maintenance of amenities either by the State or by the people themselves. The present low status of health in our country is due to poverty and ignorance of our rural population who have become apathetic through generations of woeful living.

Environment

The ingredients of a decent human environment are many. The home and its surroundings should not only provide shelter from sun, wind and rain but should provide comfort, privacy and protection against biological contagion. Water supply should be safe and adequate for drinking, cooking, washing and bathing. Clean and nutritious food and milk, hygienically prepared and stored should be available in adequate quantities to all the members of the family. The environment of the work place should be free from physical, physiological, pathological and psychological hazards. There should be reasonable facilities for the hygienic disposal of human and other wastes of the entire community without endangering pollution of soil, crop or water. Places of public resort such as festivals and fairs, places of recreation, public transportation, schools and auditoria require special attention in the provision of special hygienic amenities for the prevention of contact communicable diseases. Insects and other vectors of diseases should be eliminated from the human environment with a view to eradication of diseases transmitted by them.

Housing

Several parasitic, bacterial and viral infections are usually associated with poor housing conditions and over crowding. There is a considerable shortage of houses. More than half of the rural houses are one-roomed. Relate the density of 5.4 persons per rural home to a one-roomed house. You will realise the extent of the health problem as a result of defective and insufficient housing. If you consider the problem of cattle living together with human beings, the gravity of the health problem can be further realised.

Water Supply

The World Health Organisation (WHO) experts have estimated that nearly half of the morbidity in South East Asia region is due to water-borne diseases. Water problem has two aspects. 1. Quantity and 2. Quality. Quality is in fact more important from the stand-point of health. The water should be safe. As for the quantity, it should be adequate for cooking, drinking, washing, bathing and for the use of domestic animals. The usual sources of water supply in our rural areas are rivers, tanks, springs, canals and wells most of which are subjected to the high degree of constant pollution which under existing conditions cannot be prevented. Prevention of surface and sub-coil contamination is essential.

Drainage

The matter of sewerage disposal should be done in one way or other. Properly laid out and covered soakage points may be planned. Kitchen garden will help to a great extent. The pollution of water, soil, food and drinks are largely due to improper disposal of human excreta. The ideal method of disposal is of course the introduction of water carriage system. It is however impracticable in rural areas at present. Therefore it is necessary to adopt practical methods, which are cheaper and suited to our rural conditions in practices.

Wardha latrine is advisable as it costs nothing but manual labour and it is also useful as good manure to the crop. A manure pit to every house should be the objective. Most of our villagers are already adopting this idea only they are indiscriminately duping the refuse all over the backyard or on the streets. A fair sized dug out compost pit is recommended. It is worthwhile to draw attention to the fact that the provisions of water supply, drainage, disposal of night soil and other refuse are intimately related to the general problem of housing.

Control of Diseases

To control the disease disseminating vectors of mosquito, fly, flea, louse, tick, sandfly, rodent and others, it is imperative to control the environmental factors which favour their breeding, development and existence.

Mosquito Control

Mosquitoes are responsible for malaria, filariasis, etc. To the extent possible such measures as avoidance of stagnation of rain, sullage or any kind of water in pools and puddles in and around houses and villages by the simple process of filling up and other measures referred to above may be tried with advantage. DDT spraying also is to be tried.

Fly Control

Fly is responsible for the mechanical transmission of diseases, especially gastro-intestinal diseases. Fly breeds in filth and control of fly therefore depends on the efficient disposal of human excreta, animal dung, household garbage and refuse, sewage and sullage water. Provision of sanitary latrines, sanitary cow sheds, sanitary manure pits, sanitary sullage, disposal system, etc., help to prevent fly breeding to a large extent. DDT also helps in this regard.

Rat Control

Improvement of general sanitation in the home and the village will have a salutary effect on rat control. Avoidance of dumping of unwanted materials in and around the home, properly improved grain storage bins, frequent rearranging of materials in the home, the judicious use of taps should go a long way in rat control.

Food and Milk Sanitation

Problem of food sanitation in villages is not so serious as in towns. If attention is paid to such fundamental matters as the use of safe water for preparing eatables and washing utensils, avoidance of cooking and selling food articles on the edges of streets and dirty lanes, covering of food by suitable means, food insanitation can be avoided to a great extent.

Basic Education

In India education holds the premier position in the social life of the people and their development. Any investment in education is a worthy contribution and can be considered as an asset for the country for the present and for the years to come. The nature and quality of our future generation will be remarkably depending upon the quality and curriculum of the education and the methodology adopted for its imparting.

Unfortunately we are continuing our experiments, too far and too fast in the field of education, without taking heed of the effects or potential results of one or the other experiments undertaken. Many a times the content of education is divorced from reality of life and the values and the major elements in social life get diluted in the process. In this context it will be extremely important to call to memory the contribution of Gandhiji on educational thought.

Gandhiji was not an academician nor an educationist in the rigid sense of the term. But his views on education has a serious and lasting outlook towards education that could be of high value to Indian education system at all time. His contribution in this regard could be considered as the most important one to India for her social development. He had a broad outlook towards life as such and education in particular. He did not consider literacy as a synonym to education. For him, education means, 'an all-round drawing out of the best in child and man-body, mind and spirit. It is one of the means whereby man and woman can be educated. Literacy in itself is no education'. It shows that he was viewing education as a means for alround human development. He held the view that the optimum enrichment and development of personality should be achieved through education.

As a social philosopher, Gandhiji wanted education to be a powerful medium for social change and development. He was of the opinion that unless the individual change takes place the social development is impossible. Hence he gave utmost importance to character-building and reshaping of the attitudes and values. He said, 'True education does not consist in literacy, training, but in character building'. Again, 'Literary education is of no value if it is not able to build up a sound character'. From his experience, he realised that no development is possible unless attempted through self-sufficiency. So he stressed for a free and self-supporting education. Real education to him means economic self-sufficiency.

Gandhiji kept the ideal of achieving self-realisation as the ultimate aim of education. He expected the following:

1. *All-round development of the students*. 'Man is neither mere intellect, nor the gross animal body, nor the heart, nor soul alone. A proper and harmonious combination of all the three is required for the making of the whole man and constitutes the true economics of education', said Gandhiji.
2. *Cultural education*. Gandhiji said, 'Culture is the foundation; it should show itself in the smallest details of your conduct and personal behaviour. . . . Inner culture must be reflected in your speech, the way in which you treat visitors and guests and behave towards one another and your teachers and elders. Again, 'True education, is that which draws out and stimulates the spiritual, intellectual and physical faculties of the children'. He wanted to base education on indigenous culture because, otherwise, it would make the educated unfit for the service of the community and make them foreigners in their own land. He held the view that the social aim of education does not come in conflict with the individual aim. Man is to serve society and society is to help man. For the attainment of these aims, he had offered concrete methods and techniques as well. This was covered fully in the Basic Education.

Gandhiji called for a National Education Conference at Wardha on October 1937. Basic education was the outcome of this conference. He wanted to establish a Sarvodaya society in India. Basic Education alone can bring in this desired results.

The gist of the Basic Education could be presented as follows:

1. Education should be made free and compulsory for the children in the age group of 7 to 14 years.
2. Gandhiji wanted to make education self-supporting. He said, 'My

Nai Talim is not dependent, should come from the educational process itself, whatever the criticism may be, I know that the only education is that which is self-supporting'. Again, '*Nai Talim* without the self-supporting basis would, therefore, be like a lifeless body'. After the completion of seven years of free and compulsory education, the children should be capable of taking up some meaningful occupation enabling them to stand on their own foot. This will help the children develop confidence and security as well as making them realistic and productive. 'The child at the age of 14, that is after finishing a seven-year course should be discharged as an earning unit . . . you impart education and simultaneously cut at the root of unemployment', said Gandhiji.

3. Education, as Gandhiji visualised, was one which is craft-centred. In fact craft was considered as the medium for earning and development i.e., learning through craftwork and later earning through the same. It is relevant to mention that Kothari Commission also stresses the work experience in education. It further lays stress on community learning for community welfare in school and colleges.
4. Gandhiji wanted education to revolve around a teacher and not on books. He said, 'I have always felt that the true text-book for the pupil is his teacher, because children take in much more and with less labour through their ears than through their eyes'. For him, 'the teacher was to be most respected and most spiritual man in society. He should act as the true model for the student. I do not believe that this can be imparted through books. It can only be done through the living touch of the teacher'. The type of education that he visualised was based on the tacit assumption of intimate interaction between the teacher and students. Values such as co-operation, discipline, sacrifice, integrity fearlessness etc., are part of such teacher-student relationship.
5. Basic education stressed very much on discipline and not in ultimate freedom. Gandhiji said, 'No training is possible without discipline and restriction'.
6. The medium of instruction should be mother-tongue. A foreign language deprives them of the spiritual and social heritage of the nation, and renders them to that extent unfit for the service of the country. The introduction of English language by the British people blocked the development of Indian languages. The

foreigners had their own plan of exploitation in this regard. Mother-tongue, being the most simple for any child, is the easiest one to pick-up.

7. The higher Education should not be costly one and it should not be at the expense of the poor tax-payers, says Gandhiji. However, still, we could see that only the middle and upper classes are the main beneficiaries of the present education system sponsored out of the money contributed by the poor.

Technology

Gandhiji wanted to bridge the gap between rich and poor through the instrument of technology. He felt the need for the integration of industry and education. He expected the technological advancement to facilitate the over-all development of the country. However, he cautioned the nation to limit the dependence on machines so that man may not become its slave. He aimed at developing a spiritual man dedicated to truth and non-violence.

Spiritual progress of man was the primary aim of Gandhiji. All other factors were considered as ancillaries. He differed from Karl Marx, who gave importance to materialism even at the cost of spiritualism. Thus education should always lead man closer to spiritual attainment and progress. Instead of moral education Gandhiji advocated the teaching of ethical ideas.

As a champion pleader of non-violence, Gandhiji stressed the importance of *ahimsa* to be attained through education. He said, 'true education and violence are fundamentally opposed to each other and true education can be given through non-violence and this is the central idea of his education scheme'.

Students and Politics

Gandhiji was of the opinion that students should not participate in politics. To maintain the sober and serene nature of education, the interweaving of politics in education could be a blockade. Being a firm believer in Gram Panchayat, he maintained that politics will be a barrier to the development of students. It affects their concentration and leads to disgression from the studies.

State Interference

Gandhiji was not against state interference. He wanted financial assistance from the state, but the state should not interfere in the educational activities. He was fully aware of the possible consequences such an intervention could lead to. Hence he was cautioning to keep the education free from various political interference so that it can maintain its purity and independence.

Gandhiji was of the opinion that Village *Swaraj* could be achieved through *swadeshi* only. For this education was considered as an elementary pre-requisite. Hence Gandhian concept of education and his concept of *swadeshi* are interwoven. Without *swadeshi* there cannot be any meaningful national education system. The problem of educated people seeking the first opportunity to work abroad, as seen today, is definitely a proof as to why Gandhiji cautioned and stressed the concept of *swadeshi* in the field of education.

Gandhiji laid much stress on the character formation. He adhered to the principle of simple living and high thinking to be adopted and achieved through education. A luxurious life spoils the mind, making it rigid while life based on voluntary poverty and simplicity is the one most desirable. He proved this through his life.

Heeding his inner voice, Gandhiji advocated the significance of prayer. He started his programmes with prayer only; in *ashram* life prayer had its own deserving place irrespective of any particular religion. As a process of self-disciplining, he considered prayer as an important medium. As a votary of universal religion, he stressed the importance of prayer in all walks of life, particularly in education. He recommended prayer and reading or recitation of holy scriptures for inclusion in a programme of moral education.

Conscientisation of the masses is essential for any meaningful change as it prepares them with basic change in their attitudes. Gandhiji was of the opinion that to face and deal with national problems such as population, energy crisis and unemployment, the need of the hour is to make people realise the causes and consequences of these basic human problems. He was optimistic in the sense that meaningful and proper education can put effective check on such problems and thereby ensuring progress of the nation. He held the view that the students must be trained to think independently, critically and creatively. For this he stressed on the three Hs (Head, Heart and Hand) rather than three Rs (Reading, Writing and Arithmetic).

It is said that Gandhian ideas on education was not properly understood and accepted in the very land that gave birth to him. Instead of making efforts to understand his ideology in the proper perspective, many were on the look out for finding the loopholes in the scheme. In their efforts to find the errors, out of their own ignorance and lack of positive outlook, they missed the gist and true content of the scheme.

Such a critical look towards his plan of education was definitely hampering and unfortunate. The critics lacked the optimistic and constructive outlook towards achieving an ideal society as Gandhiji desired to bring in. Much against all the doubts and comments, Gandhiji says, 'I have given many things to India. But this system of education together with its technique is, I feel, the best of them. I do not think I will have anything better to offer the country'.

Education as Gandhiji perceived was a continuous and life-long process. It starts from the conception and ends with death. He has taken a broad view of education thereby freeing it from the clutches of specified institutions and throwing it open for the common man for his entire life. As a social reformer and thinker, he wanted to awaken their conscience and alert masses to fight against social evils. He was of the sole opinion that a society based on truth and non-violence alone can bring in an upliftment of all-*sarvodaya*. For this, education was a means and medium. To put it in his own words, 'Educational approach is the spearhead of silent social revolution fraught with the most serious consequences'.

Adult Education

Only a few of our leaders and national thinkers could properly identify the potentials we have and still fewer could give the clarion call for the arousal of the human potentials. Undoubtedly Gandhiji is in the forefront among the reformists and thinkers who could identify the commendable role that the people, particularly villagers, can play for the development of the nation.

Realising fully this fact, Gandhiji had the insight and courage to advocate for the promotion of literacy and education among the masses. Education is a pre-requisite for social development. Unfortunately many remain illiterate or uneducated. The climate of ignorance and illiteracy was considered as profitable one for exploitation and corruption. Poor and illiterate people were in all sense kept in darkness. It gave rise to series of social and economic problems. In country, like India, the importance of education cannot be overlooked. Experience derived from a country such as Russia gives us sufficient evidence regarding the need and significance of education.

Education is a must, and literacy as essential medium for the all-round development. Nearly 60 per cent of population in India remains illiterate. This is unfortunate while considering the role and responsibility of people in a democratic set-up. Even though crores of rupees are being spent, yet the result is not satisfactory.

Gandhiji was of the opinion that mere formal education for the children in established institutions will not solve the larger problem of illiteracy. Hence a practical plan of action was formulated to extend the benefit of education to the adult group as well, so as to bring them closer to the national level efforts for all-round progress. Thus emerged the scheme of Adult Education.

Before the introduction of Basic Education, Gandhiji advocated social or adult education in order to establish *Sarvodaya* society. He was taken up by the conviction that the elders and parents need to know reading and writing so that they can guide the younger generation properly. Remaining idle and ignorant may directly or indirectly limit the progress of their future generation. Hence he believed that adult education can fulfil this task.

Adult education stands for basic minimum education of every adult above 18 years of age. Its main aim is to prepare the individual to lead a healthy life, to work profitably and to raise his economic level through literacy by the provision of extension of education.

Once the objectives and need of educating the adult was finalised, Gandhiji wanted to start it as a project for experimenting with the Adult Education programme. Thus he entrusted Mrs. Shanta Narulkar to spread his conception of Adult Education in and around Wardha district. The results were promising.

Broadly speaking Adult Education has the following objectives:

1. Inculation of awareness among the illiterate adults.
2. Literacy and numeracy.
3. Improvement of the occupational skills.

The focus of the whole educational programme should be learning so that such a learning can lead to changes in the people. The primary function of an adult education programme is that of creating desirable changes in people. All the efforts can be of no use if such an objective is not accomplished. Therefore, unless the adult education programme has an impact upon the behaviour of the people, it will be a futile exercise. Thus it needs a clear and achievable education objectives. The teaching materials and methodology are also to be selected accordingly. The behavioural aspects of the objective of the adult education has the following factors namely thinking, feeling and acting. Adult education has many positive factors. It gives opportunities for adults irrespective of their age, state of maturity. It does not believe in formal "Classroom and lecture approach". Moreover adults can discuss in this forum varied experiences from different fields. Better group interaction and sharing of experience can foster a more effective and beneficial communication.

Conditions for Adult Learning

1. The adult must be adequately motivated to change behaviour.
2. The adult must be aware of the inadequacy of his present behaviour.
3. The adult must have a clear picture of the behaviour which he is required to adopt.
4. The adult must have opportunities to practise the appropriate behaviour.
5. The adult must get reinforcement of the correct behaviour.
6. The adult must have avail a sequence of appropriate materials.

Prior to Adult Education, India had other strategies for educating the masses. At no time were all Indians literate. In the past religious discourses, cultural activities gave a peaceful atmosphere to live. However, it did not teach them to read and write but were effective in the sense that it gave a sense of mutual co-operation and peace with contentment. Today cinema has replaced these arrangements. The ancient people though illiterate, cultivated their lands, reared their cattles, practised their handicrafts and rural industries with skills and produced wealth. Gandhiji did not want them to delink from their occupation on account of education.

In the Gandhian perspective, education is a continuous process from the womb to tomb. Every village must start life-long education centre where adults of age group 20-60 would come together every night for self-learning under a voluntary guide. They are taught the art of recycling the waste materials into usuable articles such as paper, soap, powder, candle, etc. The idea was to make them understand the principle of self-sufficiency.

Adult Education has been considered to be a highly specialised forum by Gandhiji. He considered illiteracy as one of the fundamental causes of general backwardness. Therefore, he outlined a concrete plan of Adult education for awakening the conscience of the masses and bringing them into the main stream of national development.

Gandhiji wrote, 'This has been woefully neglected by Congressmen. Where they have not neglected it, they have been satisfied with teaching illiterates to read and write. If I had charge of adult education, I should begin with opening the minds of the adult pupils to the greatness and vastness of their country. The villager's India is contained in his village. If he goes to another village, he talks of his own village as his own home. Hindustan is for him a geographical term. We have no notion of the ignorance prevailing in the villages. The villagers know nothing of foreign rule and its evils. What little knowledge they have picked up fills them with the awe the foreigner inspires. The result is the dread and hatred of the foreigner and his rule. They do not know how to get rid of it. They do not know that the foreigner's presence is due to their own weakness and their ignorance of the power they possess to rid themselves of the foreign rule. My adult education means, therefore, first, true political education of the adult by word of mouth. Seeing that this will be mapped out, it can be given without fear. I imagine that it is too late in the day for authority to interfere with this type of education; but if there is interference, there must be fight for this elementary right without which there can be no *Swaraj*. Of course, in all I have written, openness has been assumed. Non-violence abhors fear and, therefore, secrecy. Side by side with the education by the mouth will be the literacy education. This is itself speciality. Many methods are being tried in order to shorten the period of education. A temporary or permanent board of experts may be appointed by the working committee to give shape to the idea here adumbrated and guide the workers. I admit that what I have said in this paragraph only points the way but does not tell the average Congressmen how to go about it. Nor is every Congressmen fitted for this highly special work. But Congressmen who are teachers should find no difficulty in laying down a course in keeping with the suggestions made herein'.

In 1944 Gandhiji wrote, 'Adult education of my conception must make men and women better citizens all-around. To work out the syllabus and to organise the work of adult education is more difficult task than preparation of the seven year's course for children. The common central feature of both will be the imparting of education through the village craft. Agriculture will play a very important part in adult education under the basic scheme. Literacy instruction must be there. Much information will be given orally. There will be books, more for the teachers than the taught. We must teach the majority how to behave towards the minority and *vice versa*. The right type of adult education should teach neighbourliness and cut at the very root of untouchability and the communal problem. . . . The particular industry which is to serve as the medium of instruction will be determined by the local condition in each place. For instance, people in a village might tell you that they are interested in agriculture but they are not interested in the spinning wheel. In that case, you will choose the former as the medium of instruction. You could make a beginning by taking a census of its cattle. For instance, I find that almost everyone in *Sevagram* has a bullock and a bullock-cart. It seems wasteful'.

Vinoba also believed in such an educational scheme and recommended series of concrete ideas to make the endeavour a real success. He suggested the one hour school for the children below 15 years. The illiterate adults will assemble in a common place at about 8 p.m. everyday after their day's work and supper. They are to be trained in community prayers and *bhajans* and stories from epics are told, followed by discussions on village problems and its solutions. Thus, the adult's general awareness regarding the day-to-day affairs improve.

To quote Vinobas 'In every village there should be a regular reading of instructive literature. Just as we need food everyday in order to live, similarly the mind must receive its food. While bread is the food for the body, knowledge is the food for the mind. Villagers should organise the reading of *Tulsi Ramayana*, the Autobiography of Gandhiji and *Gita Pravachan*. The peasant works the whole day and has no time to read for himself. If he reads, his eyes get affected. Hence every village should organise public reading. If they cultivate the habit of listening to good things their village will change in no-time'.

In line with Gandhiji's concept of Adult education, a concrete national programme was formally inaugurated on 2nd October, 1978. This is termed as National Adult Education Programme (NAEP). According to Government's policy statement, while emphasising acquisition of literacy, skills were also to be relevant to the environment and learner's need; flexible regarding duration, time, location, instructional arrangements, diversified in regard to curriculam, teaching and learning materials and method, and systematic in all aspects of organisation.

The outline of NAEP suggested the following types of programme to be organised under the scheme: literacy with assured follow-up; conventional functional literacy; functional literacy supportive of a dominant development programme; literacy with learning-cum-action groups; literacy for conscientisation and formation of organisation of the poor.

NAEP is a highly significant welfare idea in the present set-up in India. No educational movement after Basic education propounded by Gandhiji has offered more promise for the future in India than this. For the proper and effective participation of people in the socio-political circles, literacy is a must. In a democratic country like ours, its need is much more. It can further liberate the people from the threshold of outworn customs, superstition and tradition which remain important causes of their backwardness.

Considering the significance of NAEP in India, one could easily arrive at the need for more comprehensive and committed effort in improving the programmes. It could be facilitated further through adult education research. Specific and properly co-ordinated plane should fill in research gaps. It would be desirable to have more collaboration among adult educators to set priorities collectively and to arrange integrated research projects so that we can concentrate on central rather than peripheral problems in adult education.

The results of adult literacy is yet to be improved. Many factors are quoted as reasons for the slow progress. Many times, the programmes are conceived merely to develop abilities to read and write. The common Indian villager does not realise the importance of reading and writing. Literacy in the sense of mere reading and writing cannot be an end in itself. It has to be linked with certain function, skills and vocations. Thus emerged the reconceptualisation of adult literacy as functional literacy.

In India, research in adult education remains meagrely done whereas many more research avenues remain unexplored. Universities can play a crucial role in propagating the message of adult education as well as undertaking action research programmes in all related topics. Those who have given serious thought in this direction agree on certain points such as the general appropriateness for a university to provide adult education in fields which has academic strength and can evoke depth and maturity of response associated with University education. Further, the universities can take up experimental projects and give advice and leadership to other organisations working in adult education. The Universities should keep its value alive in the community of which it is a part and within that community it should encourage the people to participate actively in this national venture. Mass media should be fully made use of.

A review of literature in the areas of adult education shows that many of the studies so far conducted are in the form of status studies, assessing the situation, especially with reference to the programme of social education and literacy in action. The findings are relevant in regard to personnel methods, materials, wastage of efforts, etc. However, methodological sophistication is highly warranted. More experimental, coordinational, evaluative and follow-up studies, involving indepth case study are required to arrive at more useful and conclusive references.

The Government has also formulated the following policies and strategies for better implementation of the programme:

1. The Government of India will continue to provide grants-in-aid to voluntary organisations working in the field of adult education. However, keeping in view the criticism voiced earlier about infiltration of the programme by voluntary organisations having communal leanings, stricter scrutiny will be made of the voluntary organisations seeking Government funds for their programmes to eliminate communal elements infiltrating the programme. For this purpose certain norms have been prescribed by the Government which have been circulated to all concerned. The procedure for giving grants to these organisations have also been modified to ensure better performance and proper utilisation of funds by the voluntary agencies.
2. Larger participation of students in the adult education programme will be enlisted. Necessary modalities for the same are being worked out and will be sent to all concerned in due course.
3. According to 1981 Census, 243 districts out of 402 have literacy rate below the national average. The literacy rate is also very low amongst women, scheduled castes, scheduled tribes, migrant labourers and others weaker sections of the society. Concerted

efforts will be made to organise programmes for wider coverage of these target groups and areas so as to improve literacy position amongst them. As contemplated in the Sixth Five Year Plan Document, it would be the endeavour of the Government to take steps for covering 100 per cent adult literates in the age group 15-35 (numbering about 10.74 crores) by the year 1990.

4. Special attention would be paid to the organisation of adult education programme for the physically handicapped. As the past experience in organisation of adult education programme for the physically handicapped people is very limited, a few pilot and experimental projects will be taken up as soon as possible.
5. The Adult Education Programme would be implemented in three phases as recommended by the Kothari Review Committee. The programmes of post-literacy and follow-up will be activated and strengthened to avoid relapse into illiteracy of neo-literates and induct them in the process of self-learning.
6. If the instructor organises classes for the second and the third phases also, he would be given extra remuneration the details for which would be worked out shortly.
7. The National Board of Adult Education would be reconstituted to advise Government on formulation of policies and programmes of adult education and for co-ordination in their implementation. Its responsibility would also include support to development of the state resource centres, monitoring, evaluation and research and general improvement on the quality and coverage of programme.
8. Steps will also be taken to activise all existing State Boards of Adult Education.
9. Suitable schemes will be formulated to support traditional and folk arts *per se* and also their fuller and wider use in the furtherance of literacy and adult education programmes.
10. The potential of electronic media particularly the telecasting network available through INSAT would also be utilised for the adult education programme.

Considering education as a social investment, one could aptly comment on the need for a greater integration in adult education programme. It is now necessary to review the programme fully, particularly in the event of governmental initiative and assistance channelled so much to promote the adult literacy. NAEP could be rightly considered as the extension of Gandhian ideology to make more and more people of India literate, conscious and educated. There is need for more commitment and devotion on the part of authorities and teachers for a meaningful implementation of the national adult education programme.

Uplift of Women

Man inevitably exhibits some feminine qualities and woman a few male propensities. Artha Nari in Hindu theology is a typical example of man-woman combination in every human being.

Gandhiji was a very shy lad. According to the custom then prevalent he was forced to marry when he was mere thirteen years old. His wife happened to be just six months older than he. Naturally the boy husband had to exercise his authority over his wife. Sometimes he treated her harshly expecting implicit obedience for all his commands. But he was not able to turn his better half to his likes and dislikes.

Gandhiji spent three years in England for getting his Bar-at-law degree. He was able to observe the role played by the English women in their social set up. Again in South Africa he moved with a few European ladies during his famous *satyagraha* movement. He was able to appreciate how they contributed equally with men to the general causes under all circumstances without being the least disturbed. Lady Doke was his first biographer. Mrs. Alexander, wife of the Superintendent of Police, helped him from being mortally wounded by the South African crowd of whites. He was all praise for Miss Schlesin, his German Secretary for her moral courage and efficiency at work. All these people cast their indirect influence on him to change his concept of women.

The year 1906 is very significant in the life of Gandhiji. He decided, soon after his return from service in Zulu Rebellion, to become a *Brahmachari*, throughout his life. His wife also gave him the green signal with her ready acceptance of his suggestion. For the first time he felt that Kasturba was his equal. He began to treat her as his sister associated in his humanitarian work. The superiority complex so far predominant in his mind completely vanished from the scene. The companionship Kasturba gave him in his tumultuous life always stood him in good stead and helped him tide over many a crisis very smoothly and purposefully. Indeed his 37th year was a turning point in his revolutionary life to make him a *Mahatma*.

The South African Satyagraha has three distinct phases. In the first phase hundreds went to jail opposing the move of the Government to get the finger prints of all the ten fingers of the Indians. In the next they were imprisoned for setting ablaze their passports in bonfire. Thousands participated in this novel way of protest. But when Supreme Court Judge gave a verdict that only marriages performed according to the Christian rites were recognised in South Africa, the Indian women took it as a challenge to their chastity and womanhood. This curious judgment at once made the wives of the South African Hindus, Muslims and Parsis as concubines and deprived their progeny from inheriting their family properties. The women-folk who had been so far away from the active scene of *satyagraha* had no other go than to jump into the fray with all their might.

Kasturba was the first to offer her services in this fight for natural justice to the women's cause. Gandhiji never compelled anyone to join the *satyagraha* but only educated them with facts and figures of the case including the sufferings they had to bear in the South African jails. Yet, the Indian women came in large numbers in the famous natal-transvaal March organised by Gandhiji. Unlike in India anyone crossing the border of one State in the Union of South Africa had to do so with a valid permit. So Gandhiji asked the miners and their families on strike to march into Transvaal territory without any visa. The police did not arrest the 5000 men, women and children until they neared the Tolstoy Farm, 30 km from Johannesberg. The *Padayatra* squad had only one pound bread and an ounce of sugar as their rations and they even had to cross fast-flowing rivers on the way. On one such occasion it so happened that a child carried by its mother on her shoulders was swept away by the furious floods and she without making the usual hue and cry continued her march quite undisturbed. Such was the morale of the women *satyagrahis* under Gandhiji's banner in South Africa.

With the aid of his German friend, Kallenbach, he purchased some lands with a small farm house and orchards in it and settled the uncared families with great concern. It was a mini India with unity in diversity of languages, religions and races. He made the men, women and children earn their bread through labour and live in unison forgetting their castes and customs. Thus in the Tolstoy Farm Gandhiji leant the techniques of mingling with the people of different sexes, religions, traditions, etc., and shaping them into citizens of the world.

During Champaran *Satyagraha* in Bihar, Gandhiji had an occasion to see the naked poverty of the women folk. He had been to the village where Kasturba was moving with the local people. In one of the houses a woman came out to see Gandhiji. Immediately she went in and in a few minutes another appeared on the scene. Soon after her exit, a third woman came out of the house. Gandhiji began to think why all of them should not come out at a time. On enquiry through Kasturba, he came to know that they had only one sari to wear in the family. No wonder then that he wanted to clothe all the people through the *Charkha* he rediscovered through the unceasing efforts of that remarkable lady, Gangabehn Mazumdar. It was thus a woman who helped Gandhiji to locate the *Kamadenu* of his Constructive Programme. Khadi which started in 1920s as relief measure, passed the stage of providing a living wage in 1930s and has now reached the point of realising its pragmatic philosophy stage of the livery of freedom at all levels of living. His great concern for the recovery of women from their pitiable plight made Gandhiji to introduce Khadi and Village Industries scheme in this country.

Gandhiji was dead against child marriages. He never thought that a child widow is a widow in its true perspective. So he strongly advocated, in the teeth of opposition from the *Sanatana* Hindus, for the remarriages of the so-called widows and quoted from *Sastras* that they are acceptable to reason and dignity of womanhood.

From time immemorial man has treated woman as a weaker sex. But Gandhiji fully knew that there was no such complex in the Vedic times. The inferior status of woman was thrust upon her by Manu and his followers. They opined that woman, when young must be protected by her parents, when matured should be under the custody of her husband and when old under the support of her children. Gandhiji definitely attacked the view that a woman is a toy of lust and that her duty is to bear child as a machine. He had liberated our women folk from their doldrum and put them on the wheel of national progress and prosperity.

Gandhiji considered woman as the other half of man. Naturally he despised the idea of getting dowry at the time of marriage. In fact, he never wanted women to wear ornaments to increase their beautiful look. He desired that they should raise themselves through dedicated service to the needy. So he blessed such of the persons to marry a Harijan. He conducted the weddings of Jayaprakash Narayan and Acharya Kripalani on the condition that they would remain *Brahmacharis* and treat their wives as companions only.

When Kasturba died at Aga Khan Palace in Poona, Gandhiji was at her bed side. He had her head on his lap and began to reminisce his 62 long years of married life. He earmarked nearly Rs.10 million worth donated money in remembrance of Kasturba for the Kasturba Memorial Trust and specifically said in it that this sum should be spent on the uplift of rural women. Kasturba Gram at Indore is the head quarters of this organisation which aims at training rural women for the various national tasks of rural reconstruction.

Education in Health and Hygiene

It is important to emphasise the importance of keeping the body and mind in a fit condition. To this end regular habits, a health-giving balanced diet, daily exercise, work, and above all a life of self-restraint are needed.

Many of us do not cultivate regular habits or keep to regular hours for work, sleep, food, etc. What we eat is often according to what is good to taste without regard to what is good for our bodies. We forget that we should eat in order to live. In the case of poor people a balanced diet is not possible, but the well-to-do and middle classes need to pay great attention to this important factor in their lives. Where the poor fall ill through lack of nourishing food the well-to-do suffer from diseases due to over eating. It should be within the capacity of each one of us to regulate our diet according to our needs. The simpler the cooking, the more easily digestible is our food. Grains, rice, pulses, vegetables, onions, and fruits such as papaya, mango, banana, guava, tomato, etc., which can be easily grown even in villages and milk and its products can constitute a wholesome diet.

Those who are engaged in hard physical labour do not stand in need of any other exercise, but for those who are engaged in sedantary occupations regular exercise is essential. Youths in schools and colleges often neglect to exercise their bodies with disastrous results to both body and mind. The best exercise is of course that which enables some useful work to be performed in the course of it, but this may not be possible for everyone. Walking, healthful games or yogic exercises however, can be taken by everyone according as it suits him.

Simple food, clean living and regular exercise are not only health-giving but morally uplifting. For clean living a life of self-restraint is essential. However much a man may regulate his food and exercise he cannot really be termed healthy if he indulges in *vice* and has no control over his passions. Such control is impossible without a control on the mind. Purity of mind depends to a large extent on the nature of food and exercise on takes, the type of life one leads, the company one keeps and the books one reads. Companions and literature should be chosen with the same care as food and exercise. A person who is sound in body and mind can influence and inspire others while his opposite will infect his environment with evil habits. It is essential, therefore, for workers to lead pure and healthy lives so that they may be able to spread the gospel of health and hygiene and thereby bring wealth and happiness to their neighbours.

Provincial Language (Mother-tongue)

The constructive programme of Gandhiji is an alround programme. For, it covers all the aspects of life individually and collectively. It is well known that every child begins speaking his mother-tongue. It grows through it and help others to understand and follow it. Gandhiji included mother-tongue in his constructive programme in order to awaken the people to see the need for the same.

Language is a step forward in the process of our civilisation. One of the main differences between the human beings and animals is our ability to speak. It is only the art of our speech that makes others understand what we aim at. Through speech we are able to express our innermost thoughts and feelings.

Every country has its own languages. In India Sanskrit and Tamil are the oldest of the languages. Though we call India as a country, it is proper to call it as a sub-continent. For everyone of its states is having its individual language, sometimes quite different and on most occasions slightly different from one another. This multi-linguism is a factor to be reckoned with in matters national. In fact we have divided our country into linguistic provinces. The idea behind this move was that every language will flourish and help others in coming up. But what do we see now? Everywhere there is tension in the name of languages. The whole thing has arisen because the people of the concerned states have not understood the purpose behind this form of division. Instead of loving and patronising their language they have become mad after it. This fadism has caused a lot of headache to the Centre as well as the State governments. It is high time that we rethink over this perilous situation and solve it peacefully and sagaciously.

Mother-tongue is as good as mother's milk to the child. If a mother suckles her baby with her breast milk, it is easily digestible and healthy. The baby grows very fast and in a natural way absorbing our traditions. In the same manner if a child learns through its mother tongue, it learns quickly and effectively. It is able to understand facts, think over them and build upon them. This situation was altered by the British Government through its thrusting English upon all. In spite of the fact that we are free country for more than 42 years, we are yet to change this British model in our educational system. Added to this it has become the fashion of the day to learn only through English. Every mother seems to feel pleased when her little child calls her mummy instead of *Aayi*; not knowing that mummy refers to a tanned corpse. This epidemics has infected even the poorest of the rural parents.

There is no better fitted person than Gandhiji to speak for mother-tongue. Once Gandhiji was in London. He was felicitated by the Gujarati students prosecuting high studies in English. They read out their welcome address in English. Gandhiji was touched to the quick. So he addressed them in Gujarati only thereby pointing out that they should have expressed their feelings in their mother-tongue. The first book he wrote was in Gujarati only. He edited the Indian opinion in Gujarati and English. He wrote his auto-biography in Gujarati only. He would not speak to any stranger in India in any other language than his mother-tongue unless he comes to know that he does not know it. Such was his loyalty to his mother-tongue based upon sound psychological principle.

Gandhiji thought in 1937 that India would become free sooner than others expected. His attention immediately turned towards the education of our children. He convened a National Conference at Wardha. There he was able to influence the assembled educationists on the medium of instruction in basic schools. Therefore, the second resolution said that medium of instruction will be the mother-tongue or the regional language. Gandhiji was of the opinion that all should learn through their mother-tongue at all levels of education. If this procedure had been followed by us, we should have by this time produced world famous stalwarts in all fields from our villages. If the same is adopted in courts and offices, peoples' participation will be full to the brim adding to the efficacy of democracy. So we can understand now the importance of mother-tongue in the constructive programme.

National Language

Every nation has got its own national language. Its growth depends upon how the programme of national language is carried out. Gandhiji, therefore, included national language in his constructive programme in order to awaken the people to see the need for the same.

Gandhiji who stood for the propagation of knowledge through mother-tongue also took into consideration the welfare of our nation. He fully knew that a good number of Indian languages were as old as the hills. He was also aware that they have a rich literature that can be applied to all fields of life. It was also known to him that India has two main groups of languages viz., the Dravidian and Aryan languages. Under the Dravidian language groups Tamil is the first followed by Telugu, Kanada, Malayalam and Tulu. Almost all the Aryan languages came under one head Sanskrit. Also these languages have a common script i.e., Nagari script. Moreover, he fully knew that a vast majority of the northern people can easily understand the various languages that are in use in their parts. Another factor which influenced his decision to choose the national language for India was his concern for the Muslims who are next in population to the Hindus in this land of Bharat. So he suggested Hindustani as the *Lingua Franca* of our country. For Hindustani is a combination of Sanskrit, Persian and Urdu which can be easily understood by all the sections of the community. So he said that Hindustani can be written and studied in both Nagari and Urdu scripts. Again he also made it compulsory for the participants in the AICC meetings whether they belonged to the North or the South or the West or the East to speak in the common languages. Naturally those who took part in our Freedom Movement learnt Hindustani willingly and conversed in it. In order to facilitate the members from the South especially from Tamil Nadu to learn the language he started Dakshin Bharat Hindi Prachar Sabha and made its headquarters Tiruchi.

As Gandhiji was a *Karma Yogi*, he made all these arrangements to popularise the national language. When the Congress ministries formed the Government in 7 States, soon after 1937 election, they introduced Hindi as a language of study in schools. Besides many people voluntarily studied Hindi and passed examinations conducted by the Hindi Prachar Sabha. Generally there was a feeling among the Indians to take it as a privilege to know and speak Hindi freely. But in course of time it was rather unfortunate political trends took a bad turn in Tamil Nadu against studying Hindi as a subject in schools. Pandit Nehru, the then Prime Minister of India took a softened attitude towards this Anti-Hindi Movement in Tamil Nadu. A youth in Tamil

Nadu has to remain without a working knowledge of Hindi. This situation is standing in the way of National Integration and Political solidarity.

The Constituent Assembly has already chosen 14 languages as national languages. Among them Tamil and Hindi find a place apart from English. The educational set up for the country says that at the secondary stage the three-language formula must be practised in all the schools of the nation. This is in accordance with the wishes of Gandhiji. All those who are born in India can move freely to any part of India in order to transact business officially and in trade. For them at least a working knowledge in Hindi will be a great asset.

National language simply means link language of a particular multi-lingual nation state. Nobody can deny the need for such a link-language. Further we should also think in terms of a Universal language which would unite the humankind. We have to live rooted in our own culture but at the same time we are members of this sub-continent and the world. Some misrepresent Gandhiji as a narrow linguistic fanatic and a supporter of Hindi imperialism. He is the earliest to support the mother-tongue and encourage multi-linguism. Humankind can achieve unity only in diversity and co-existence.

Economic Equality

There is no gain-saying the fact that an immense economic inequality prevails in present-day society. Not only are some countries much richer than others but even in the same country there are gross inequalities between individuals as also between sections of society. England and America as countries are vastly richer than India. Even in those countries, however, there are rich millionaires in contrast to the poor daily labourer who has to eke out an existence with the help of unemployment doles in dull seasons. In our own country we have the spectacle of a palace side by side with a hovel. Only in our country there are many more hovels than palaces. We know too that all wars and the most ghastly world war raging today have as their root cause the rivalry between nations for the possession of wealth and land. These will certainly continue so long as the present basis of society and outlook on life persist. Existing inequalities must, therefore, be removed, if peace and happiness are to reign over the earth. Attempts to achieve this end have been made by means of violent revolution. It remains to be seen whether what has been attained in this way will last if the violent force which brought it into being were to be removed.

The most stable and lasting equality will certainly be that which is not imposed from outside but which grows from within as a result of voluntary control of the acquisitive and exploiting tendency in man. Such a change in outlook requires a training of the mind of the individual, and if the effort to bring it about were undertaken on a nation-wide scale, it would certainly be possible, though undoubtedly the task is fraught with difficulty. But such a state of mind can only come into being in a society based on non-violence. All men are not endowed with the same nature nor with an equal amount of talent, intelligence, and capacity for work. In present day society these inequalities are aggravated and increased by artificial social advantages or disadvantages of birth, education, income, etc. Force may remove artificial social conditions, but it cannot equalise the natural gifts of individuals. These gifts can be utilised either for the benefit of the individual or for the service of all. The society which is based on violence will naturally utilise them for the aggrandisement of the individual or the particular section of society or the country to which he belongs. In a society based on non-violence they will be utilised for the benefit of all-but such a society has still to be established. Existing inequalities have to be minimised and finally removed in a non-violent manner. How can this be accomplished?

It is individuals who must make the beginning and spread the doctrine by their example. We must get rid of the notion that health and happiness depend on the riches we possess. We must realise that it is a moral duty to spend a minimum on our essential requirements and to hold the surplus in trust for the general good. 'Plain living and high thinking' do uplift, and the leaven of a simple and contented life among all workers in particular will definitely spread. Social honour or status based on character and service. The state may work towards this end while our ideal is in the making by judicious laws and taxation which encourage the removal of inequalities. But in a non-violent society the state will rarely, if ever, have need to interfere. While we are not masters in our own land we have to work as much as we can on the voluntary basis. Capitalists and factory owners may start with giving better wages and amenities of life to the workers, e.g. the wherewithal to supply themselves with good health-giving food and sufficient clothing, suitable living quarters, education for their children and healthy recreation and cultural facilities for them and those dependent on them. They may go further and divide the profits with the labourers. They may make the profits available for the country at large after retaining what is sufficient for their own requirements. Zamindars should treat their tenants fairly and justly and spend surplus incomes on the latter's vital requirements. The same applies to lawyers, doctors, etc. If all, who can, pool their surplus resources for the benefit of the masses, an immense beginning towards bringing in an equitable order will have been made. But the chief thing for the monied men is to limit their expenses so as to bring them on a level as far as possible with what should be possible for a labourer in an ideal society.

Kisan

India is a land of plenty where poor people live. This is indeed a paradox scarcely needing any proof. The reasons for this unhappy state of affairs are too many to narrate. But we cannot afford to wait for long to redeem this pitiable situation. It was left to Gandhiji to come to our rescue and he readily responded to the nation's call quite intelligently and with apt remedial measure. Such a one is Constructive Programme which should be earnestly practised by all right thinking and nation loving citizens of India.

Agriculture has been the nectar of Indian civilisation from time immemorial. Our forefathers took it as a way of life and not as a business or trade as it has come to stay now in this vast country. They derived immense pleasure in growing vegetables, corns, cotton, sugar cane, sesame, groundnuts, etc., in their fields, as they immediately fulfilled the needs of their neighbours, too. They personally took part in the various agricultural operations without much ado and enjoyed robust health and sound mental hygiene. They exchanged their products and encouraged barter system in a very natural manner. As they could not keep their cereals long, they distributed them to the needy poor who where always grateful to their benefactors and well-wishers. There was cordial relationship between the land owners and the landless labourers. So the latter put in their mettle to produce as much as they could unlike their modern counterparts who go by labour laws and other prerogatives. Peace prevailed in the rural areas accounting for perfect understanding among the individuals and groups. This was the condition of our villages before the advent of the British rule in India.

To make our villages self-sufficient in food we should adopt the following technique with care and devotion. First of all we should take into consideration the total population of the area. We should calculate the quantity of cereals and pulses needed for this number on the basis of providing them with balanced diet. The Gram Sabha should then decide the acreage for cultivating the required quantity and help the farmers in reaching the target of production through adopting safe and harmless methods of cultivation. Preference must be given to the use of tank silt, dung and urine of cattle besides green manure and *neem* cakes. Only in extraordinary circumstances we should resort to the chemical manures or fertilisers. The procedure of adopting Nature's cycle for enriching our soil and increasing the quality and quantity of our products is to be dinned into the ears of our agriculturists. As the easily and readily available manures are used as in-puts, the cost of production will come down enabling all sections of the people to get the benefit of the procedure. Moreover a good number of diseases that afflict our modern society due to the supply of polluted food stuffs will disappear from the scene.

Labour

Labour employed in factories is a group which has been organised in Trade Union. It is a small group compared with peasants. But being concentrated in industrial cities it is easy of approach and organisation. Being engaged in handling machinery and tools requiring intelligence, it is supposed also to possess more intelligence, as a class than peasants. There is no harm in organising labour for the benefit of labour, but they must not be exploited for political purposes. As in the case of Kisans much of the constructive programme is bound to benefit and should be worked among them. Trade Unions are necessary to secure for labour just and fair conditions of work and social amenities, but sometimes they are formed solely for organising strikes for creating trouble. While strikes are necessary if the employer is unreasonable and unbending, they should be resorted to only in the last instance when every other method for getting fair play and justice has failed. The guidance and help of good workers among labour is very essential. Gandhiji has claimed that the Ahmedabad Labour Union founded by him is a model for all labour. Workers should study its history and constitution and try to bring such unions into being wherever possible.

Uplift of Adivasis

Gandhiji lived for a definite objective in his life. He aimed to wipe tear from every eye. India, being one of the oldest countries of the world, has a good number of aboriginals called Adivasis. As *Sarvodaya* includes *Antyodya*, he included the uplift of Adivasis as one of the items of his broad-based Constructive Programme. This comes under his social philosophy. There are about 100 million adivasis in different parts of the country. They are the most backward in every respect and still remain uncivilised. But they are capable of contributing a lot to the total welfare of this great nation. As they are hardy people, they can put in physical work for a considerable part of the day thereby increasing our over all production.

Our mountains are rich in very valuable trees, medicinal herbs and plants, gums, resins, etc. If our adivasis population is properly educated how to utilise the available raw materials in their neighbourhood, they will certainly produce articles of exquisite beauty worth crores of rupees. As it is, the sophisticated town dwellers in their lustful mood have spread veneral diseases among these innocent and illiterate people. So they die of diseases incurable and nauseating, making their living very miserable and pathetic. They should be taught the art of living a healthy life. They have traditional rivalries among their sects and often kill themselves due to their internal feeds.

There is nothing wasteful in things created by God. Everything has its own place in the comity of things. If properly motivated, each will contribute its mite to the good of the community. So Khadi and Village Industries Programme needs must find a place in the hill areas to make the adivasis earn their living with respect. This is the reason why Gandhiji started the Adim Jati Sevak Sangh in 1930s with Thakkar Bapa as its secretary followed by V.N. Dhebar for a long time.

Lepers

Leprosy is a typical disease usually prevalent in the equatorial regions. It is one of the most dreaded diseases of the world. In olden days we in India considered it as a sinner's disease. So in Kerala and other parts of our country the lepers were removed far away from the houses. The word Leper in English language also refers to an outcaste. From these we can easily understand the fearful nature of this worst disease.

Leprosy in Mythology

Our mythology, too, abounds in stories pertaining to the lepers. For example, every Sanatana Hindu woman knows how Nalayini with exquisite devotion attended on her leprous husband and even went to the extent of carrying him in a basket to a Devadasi's house in order to fulfil her duties as a woman of rare chastity. In Tamil Nadu we have heard the story of Lord Arunagiri who became a leper due to his detestable habits and was converted into a great devotee of Lord Muruga by saving him from certain death when he jumped down from Tiruvannamalai temple tower. These stories tell us that this cruel disease can be cured only by God's grace and not by any medicines.

Gandhiji's Early Touch with Leper

The teenager Gandhiji had an occasion to meet a pious leper in his house while attending on his bed-ridden father. He was Ladha Maharaj who was known for his recovery from leprosy by his mere chanting the name of Rama. This fact is beautifully narrated by Gandhiji in his autobiography. Perhaps this incident in his early life might have made him think about leprosy and its treatment.

Gandhiji's Natural Aptitude for Nursing the Sick

Gandhiji was a very shy lad in his school days. He used to run away from the school at the stroke of the last bell and immediately began to nurse his father ailing from fistula. Thus he cultivated the habit of helping the sick persons even in his early age. When he was in South Africa, he formed the Indian Ambulance Brigade to serve voluntarily during the Boer war and Zulu Rebellion. During these periods of selfless service he was able to identify himself with the suffering people and offer them help at the most needed hour. It was in South Africa that he became a *Brahmachari* in order to volunteer fully for public service. He also learnt Nature cure so that he could not depend on a doctor for relief from physical and mental agony. Actually when his wife Kasturba was in labour pains, he acted as her mid-wife and helped her safely deliver their 4th son, Devadoss. On another occasion when Kasturba refused even in her worst condition of health to take in beef soup, Gandhiji carried her on his shoulders to his house and treated her as per nature cure method and helped her recover soon.

Again when his 2nd son, Manilal was affected by Typhoid in Bombay, he completely depended on God and nature cure system to make him live throughout his life as the strongest of his four sons. He treated the patients among the inmates of Tolstoy farm in South Africa and Sabarmati and *Sevagram* in India with the help of earth, water, air, fire and space. So, it is evident that Gandhiji had a natural aptitude for nursing the sick.

Parchure Sastri at Sevagram

One day when Gandhiji was in Sevagram Ashram, a leper suddenly appeared before him. He was none other than Parchure Sastri, a well known Sanskrit Scholar. Gandhiji was astonished to see him in such a miserable state. He asked him to stay in the ashram. But the inmates were murmering against his stay there. They openly told Gandhiji that they were afraid of becoming lepers themselves through his presence. Gandhiji respected their feelings and housed him in a hut opposite to his own. Soon after morning prayer he used to visit that hut and clean his wounds with his own hands. Thus he had a chance to tend a really suffering leper. So he began to study the causes for this disease. He refered to books on leprosy, consulted experts in the field and indigenous *vaidyas*. Consequently he was able to start a relief centre for the patients of this wasting disease at Dattapur near Wardha. There are nearly 300 lepers living as a community. One of the disciples of Gandhiji volunteered to look after this strange group of persons. He very soon became an expert in treating them. After halting the growth of leprosy among them he in fact rehabilitated them in the same compound. We will be immensely surprised to find the lepers working like the bees in a beehive. They grow cotton, weave beautifully, spin on *charkhas* and do similar easy things that produce the daily necessaries of life. This is a place worth visiting by any one interested in the welfare of the afflicted people. Why? The disease is first arrested by suitable treatment. Then the somewhat relieved patients are being given opportunities to earn their bread through undertaking activities suited to their nature and ability. The idea that when once one becomes a leper, one is a burden to the society and a constant nuisance to the pedestrians and onlookers has been removed root and branch through settling them for leading a normal social life. Psychologically the lepers feel happy over their ability to maintain themselves through their own efforts and lead a healthy community existence based on cooperation. They start their morning with Sarvodaya Prayer, participate in their community work and engage themselves in their respective occupations. Thus they lead an *ashram* life in Dattapur on constructive lines.

Facts about Leprosy

Why did Sevagram community not permit Parchure Sastri to live in the *ashram*? The fears of the inmates were illfounded. They were of the opinion that leprosy is the most contagious disease and the most incurable. But Gandhiji had an open mind. Modern science has proved beyond doubt that there are two stages in leprosy. Leprosy is said to be contagious only at the initial stage of the patient having skin thickened in the face and in the back with very shining appearance. There may be patches in the body, too. When such a person not knowing his infirmity moves freely with the people, especially with children below six years of age, he unwittingly spreads his disease to the urchins. The germs take root in their bodies slowly and appear as rashes after more than twenty or thirty years when everybody is shocked to see the symptoms of the disease. The best way to avoid it is not to allow little children mingle with the suspected patients.

Leprosy under Constructive Programme

When leprosy matures, it affects the fingers and toes and disfigures our countenance. We shed our nails and fleshy parts slowly inviting flies and mosquitoes to surround us always. Naturally others feel ill at ease for even looking at them and they run away from the scene contemptuously. The patient who needs our sympathy is at a loss to find that even his kith and kin have deserted him once and for all. Can there be a worse hellish situation in life? The fact is that this stage is the most harmless. What the patient requires is compassion from the public and a safe place to live in. Father Damien of the United States worked for years in the company of the Philippine lepers and he himself later contacted the disease falling a prey to it at the end. His services are recognised the world over. Later Christian Missionaries tried to follow him by establishing separate hospitals for the lepers. Mother Teresa has won international laurels through her undaunted and disinterested service to the persons of this nature. But it was left to Gandhiji to add leprosy relief under his famous Constructive

Programme and make it the concern of all interested in the welfare of the suffering humanity.

Hind Kust Nirvan Sangh

Gandhiji was a great humanist. He was a pragmatic philosopher. He lived a full life in conjunction with his objective in life. His goal was to wipe tear from every eye. So he formed one standing organisation under the name 'Hind Kust Nirvan Sangh' so that even after his death this humanitarian work will be carried out by his progeny. He chose the correct persons to man his movements. Prof. Jagadisan was made the Secretary of this sangh and he toured the entire part of the country propagating the truth behind leprosy and the relief measures suggested by Gandhiji. The same may be easily carried on by other voluntary agencies in the country to relieve the distressed in this field.

Problems of the Disabled

Liberal estimates show at least 10 per cent of the world population suffer from various disabilities of permanent nature. This includes mental retardation, mental illness, blindness, leprosy, etc. Further the problems of the deserted aged people and orphan children are of giant dimension. Gandhiji made significant contribution in serving the lepers.

Students

Gandhiji was a wholesome personality. He thought that every God's creation is with a definite purpose. He never wanted that anyone should be left out in the reconstruction of the nation. So he included students among his list of items mainly under his educational philosophy and partly under social, economic and political philosophies.

India is a very hoary nation. According to our *Sastras*, human life is divided into four stages. They are: 1. *Brahmacharya* 2. *Grahastha* 3. *Vanaprastha* and 4. *Sanyasa*. This is together called *Ashramadharma*. The first stage is purely reserved for students. It is the period intended for study, research and drawing inferences and generalisations. Perhaps *Brahmacharya* may sometimes extend to a period of 30 years during which the individual will remain unmarried and concentrate on attaining pure knowledge. Knowledge which is not applicable to life will be of no avail to the world. So the seeker should have an experimental attitude towards knowledge. He should also acquire the necessary skills for reaching his target. He should be ready to part with his talents so that he may be of direct use to the people around.

Students are the flowers of our generation. They are our future hopes. Our country is a Democratic Socialist Secular Republic. Our students should be made aware of each point of this statement. It is our duty to make them ideal democrats. They should understand the significance of a republic. They should also be made to know the multi-religious nature of our country.

Democracy is one of the best forms of Government. For, in it, there is scope for every citizen to contribute his mite to the total welfare of the community. Naturally every citizen has to know his rights and responsibilities. For that, proper training from early days has to be imparted to them. It is for this reason Gandhiji gave us a new type of education in 1937. It is indeed a revolution in the world of education. It aimed at the full development of the individual child. The present day schools are only factories turning out certificate holders for job that are not already there. The result is that there is unrest among the students and soul-killing competition in the society. This is indeed a bad situation prevalent in our country.

On one side millions of unemployed unproductive youths are everyday being turned out in this poor country. On the other, crores of adults remain illiterate and ignorant. This is another firy situation in a democratic country like ours. We have already said that ours is a democratic republic where the individual is the supreme consideration. In a country where there are many political parties, every party will vie with its rival to win over. If an electorate is ignorant, there is every possibility of being deceived by the party men. Gandhiji suggested social or Adult Education for the masses. He expected that it is the primary duty of every educated Indian to educate his neighbour. If each one teach one, where is the need for spending thousands of crores of rupees on Adult Education as is being done today. Here is the legitimate role of an educated unemployed youth of today.

Gandhiji lived for a definite goal in life. He said, 'I seek neither Kingdom nor Heaven nor even Salvation. All I seek is to relieve the afflicted from affliction'. He lived to wipe every tear from every eye. Thus he had a simple living and high thinking. Since he had a fixed objective in his life he corrected himself whenever he went away from his goal. So he expected that every youth should have a golden aim to live for. He wanted young men and women to grow with a specific ideal.

Gandhiji when addressing women students in Sri Lanka told them point blank that they should possess sterling character to be of any use to the society. The students may be very good at studies. They may even go to the extent of inventing things of importance. Some of them may be excellent speakers or even writers. In spite of all these merits if they do not have golden· character, every thing is lost beyond recognition. So Gandhiji wanted all students to earn good character and conduct.

To conclude we may say that:

1. a student is the hope of the humanity.
2. he should be really educated for life, through life and throughout life.
3. he should understand his environment and work for its prosperity.
4. he should practice some craft and stand on his own legs in times of need.
5. he should educate his neighbours in happy and healthy living.
6. he should become the keeper of our morals and traditions.
7. he should maintain a high ideal and simple living.
8. he should use only locally made articles in his daily life.
9. he should understand the constitution of our country and work for it faithfully.
10. he should work for communal harmony knowing fully the role of religion in our country.
11. he should practise Satya and Ahimsa in his life.
12. he should possess sterling character.

Cow Protection

In man's history, the discovery of Science of Agriculture is the greatest of all discoveries till date. This discovery revolutionised the entire life-style of Man, more than anyother discoveries did. It made an end to his nomadic life. He began to settle as a village community. He found the art of cultivation and soil conservation. With the advent of settled life in Man, he learnt the art of building houses and temples. Other arts like music, painting, writing and reading came into being. Since he found leisure due to settled life, he found time to think.

Customs and manners crept in. Religious rituals came to be observed. Ethics came to vague. Probably this should have yielded the system of family as a unit in the community life. Family began to be looked upon as sacred. It laid the foundation to modern civilisation.

Cow's part in this new dimension was very great that it gave birth to bullocks to assist man in agriculture. Bullocks helped him to plough his land, to draw water, to drive his cart, etc. Now man looked to his cow not only for milk but also for bullocks. When he was still nomadic, cow was meant for him for delicious and nutritious milk only. Thereby he switched over from hunting to rearing of cows. To him then cow was the only wealth in his possession. One's wealth was measured by the number of cows with him. One who possessed the largest number of cow was considered the respectable leader of the group. One who knew the art of cow-rearing was considered wise and as the elder in the group. This economic importance of cow became stronger after the discovery of the science of agriculture.

In Vedic period the cow began to be considered as 'Mother' because it gave milk like one's mother and it was also the mother of bullocks. The cow, being one's wealth, whereas land was plenty in those days, also served as 'exchange value' in the economic life of the village community. Cow became the back bone of the village. She was the corner stone of the village economy. Life in the village was cow-centred. There are ample instances to show that the *Gurus*, the teachers in the *Gurukula*, were paid in terms of cows as tuition fee by students. Parents gave away their daughters in marriage with cows as dowries. The ritual of giving away of cows as *'dhana'* to poor people by the rich came to practice. Cow-*dhana* was considered as the best because no other '*dhana*' would be more helpful to the beneficiaries as cow-dhana. The modern rupee and gold are fickle and often de-valued, whereas the cow as wealth is unique and study in its fidelity and utility. The spirit of sacrifice-sharing of one's wealth with others in the community began with '*Go-dhan*' and it has led to many other *dhanas* like *Bhoodan, Gramdhan, Shramdan*, etc. As a result cow was held in high esteem and worshipped as Kamadhenu, the giver of plenty.

Cow's Milk

Absolutely there is no substitute to mother's milk expect cow's milk, for it has all natural source of protein, sugar and fat almost in common with mother's milk. Even in these days of so called civilisation when

Breast-feeding is fast yielding place to bottle-feeding, cow's milk is the best one.

In *Harijan*, Gandhiji wrote under the caption 'Mother Cow' thus: Mother cow is in many ways better than the mother who gave us birth. Our mother gives us milk for a couple of years and then expects from us to serve her when we grown up. Mother cow expects from us nothing but grass and grain. Our mother often falls ill and expects service from us. Mother cow rarely falls ill. Here is an unbroken record of service which does not end with her death. Our mother when she dies, means expenses of burial or cremation. Mother cow is as useful when dead as when she is alive. We can make use of every part of her body – her flesh, her bones, her intestines, her horns and her skin and hide. Well, I say this not to disparage the mother who gives us birth, but in order to show you the substantial reason for my worshipping the cow'. At this juncture, it is to be understood that even for adults cow's milk is better than buffalo's milk. The excellant qualities of cow's milk are so obvious on the surface that no recommendation of their use for cases of debility and convalescence seems to be necessary. The superiority of cow's milk over human milk is prescribed by medical men.

The following points are the extracts taken from the letter written by Prof. Sahastrabudde of the Agricultural College, Poona, to Gandhi to say that cow-milk is better than buffalo-milk:

1. Buffalo-milk is injurious to the development of children. The fat content in cow-milk is less and so it is easily digestible.
2. Cow-milk, being easily digestible, is more beneficial to patients.
3. Cow-milk is useful for intellectual growth, mainly of children.
4. Physicians unanimously declare that cow's milk is medically superior.
5. Cow-milk is *'satvic'* whereas buffalo-milk is *'tamasik'*.

It is no wonder that cow's milk is considered holy, sacred and fit to be used in temples for *Pooja* and *Abishekam* and during religious ceremonies. It is the faith of the Hindu that the cow's milk should be the last gulp to swallow before his death and hence cow milk is poured in his mouth at the moment of one's last breath. Again, it is the custom among Hindus that cow's milk is poured on one's grave on the next day of his burial or cremation.

Cow-Dung and Urine

Cow-dung is one more major contribution of cow to humanity. It is an effective natural manure to the soil. Vinoba says, 'For our cultivation, cow-dung is like nectar to the soil in respect of fertility. The tractor will not eat grass nor give cow-dung, and on the small scale farms tractors cannot work in India'.

It is a scientific truth that cow-dung and urine have medicinal value. The research in Russia also declares that walls coated with cow-dung can protect humanity against the evil effects of atomic radiation of pollution also. Thus cow becomes the Animal of Atomic Age. Cow-dung is used as an antiseptic to prevent virus that pollutes the surroundings. This is why we have in the villages an age old custom that cow-dung mixed in water is sprinkled every morning in front of the house and in the vicinity. This is the first duty of every housewife, that she has to perform. As a ritual the places of worship are plastered with cow-dung and before performing Pooja, cow's urine is sprinkled all over the holy places. In the age of ecological pollution all over the world due to industrialisation and urbanisation, Western scientists have begun to realise the good uses of cow-dung and urine, both for medicines and for manure. At this moment, it is apt to know the basic scientific facts about natural manure and chemical manure. Natural manure such as cow-dung is like the soil's staple food, whereas chemical manure is just like a stimulant. Cow-dung is a precious natural manure which is keeping our soil fertile despite centuries of cultivation.

Apart from the use of cow-dung as the best of manure to our soil, there are multifarious other uses:

1. Cow-dung is almost the only fuel for cooking and heating which is left with the villagers once the woods in the vicinity are cut down. Electricity, gas, coal and kerosene do not reach the villagers adequately still for a considerable period, whereas cow-dung cakes are cheap and immediately available for villagers. It is estimated that cow-dung worth of Rs. 1,800 crores is available in India annually. Half of this is being used as fuel, thereby the loss of manure to that extent. Economists and scientists should carefully look into the fuel shortage in order to prevent this waste. The invention of biogas plant is a great boon, because the cow-dung used for making bio-gas does not lose its

manure value. It is further said that the dung after the use for making bio-gas, is found fit as a better manure than raw-dung. Statistics show that one cow yields dung to make bio-gas equal to the energy of two barrels of petrol every year. This means that a cow in its life gives us dung worth Rs. 3,600. In addition to this if all the cow-dung available in the country could be used for making bio-gas it could provide job for about 12 crores of people. Energy crisis will also be solved. Latest research has thrown open the possibility of preparing methane gas from cow-dung.

2. The cow-dung is not only a manure and a fuel but also an item of house building material. Houses can be constructed by the use of bricks made out of a mixture of soil and cow-dung. This is called 'garmatic brick'. There is scarcity of cement now, and it is hardly supplied to villagers. So garmatic must be considered as a very useful material in our economic planning and the cow supplying the dung must be taken special care of.
3. Cow-dung ashes and dry cow-dung cakes are very good agents for protecting grains and cereals from rotting. Garmati godowns and cow-dung ash together can keep grain safe for years because they take away the onslaught of humanity. It is a substitute for air-conditioned godowns in our warmth.
4. Cow-urine is declared as a panacea for many diseases. It has been used as medicine since long in the rural part of India.
5. Cow-dung makes the village self-sufficient at times of war and in any other emergency. It protects the village air from pollution and radiation. So cow-dung is the material of the Atomic Age.

Cow as Mother of Bullocks

Our planners are still crazy after introducing tractors for ploughing the fields. This they do in the name of modernising our agriculture. This is a short-sighted policy and it will surely end in failure. Tractors cannot be an alternative because we just cannot produce them in needed numbers. We do not have adequate fuel to run them. They are too expensive to an average Indian farmer. They plough too deep which require more water or irrigation and our villages are short of water supply. Ploughing by tractor has been declared harmful to plant growth because it pulverises the land too much, so the looseness of the soil is lost. The tractor emits the smoke which pollutes the air and the soil. Tractors are beyond the reach by small farmers and they cannot be adjusted to individual need.

As per statistics available with the Planning Commission, total requirement of tractors in India is 50 lakhs. This requires iron and steel to make them is 3 crores tons and the capital for investment in the industry is estimated to be Rs. 14,000 crores, where as our total annual production of iron and steel in India is only half crore tons. There is also fuel shortage. Now 90 per cent of our ploughing is done by bullock-drawn ploughs. Hence it is quite impossible to switch over from bullocks to tractors.

Even today there are about two crores of bullock ploughs and one and a half crores of bullock carts. For this we need 12 crores of bullocks but we have 7 crores only. This proves how imminent it to protect the cows.

The Cow and Employment

The cow and bullocks are not only living tractors, they are also living fertiliser factories. Now the machinery threatens to overrun our agriculture and transport as part of so-called planning. We must have milk, more milk and still more milk. We must therefore have cows and if have cows, the bullocks will be always with us, for these we have to provide and can provide full employment only if we yoke them to the plough, to the cart and to the *ghani*. The using of tractors involves not only unemployment of bullocks but also unemployment of our fellowmen.

The present employment capacity provided by the cows and the bullocks is shown below:

Employment through ploughing	-	8.00 crores
Bullock-cart drivers	-	2.00 "
Carpenters for making ploughs and carts	-	0.13 "
Cattle-breeding	-	0.50 "
Sugar-cane pressures by bullocks	-	0.70 "
Oil *Ghani* bullocks drivers	-	0.20 "
Employment in milk production	-	2.00 "
Total		13.00 "

This is to show that such a big area of employment opportunity is at the mercy of the cow, the mother of bullocks and our cattle wealth. Since cow contributes power, transport, food, employment, manure, milk etc., we have to conclude that our economy is 'Cow-centred economy'. So we have to protect the cows.

Nature Cure

Gandhiji believed that independence is possible and meaningful only to the healthy people, healthy in the physical, mental and spiritual conditions. Only nature cure gives the complete, harmoneous health to the individual in physical, mental and spiritual levels. Nature cure is as old as the life itself. Great thinkers like Alexis Carrol, Leo Tolstoy, Hippocratus, Aldous Huxley, Bernard Shaw and Gandhiji showed the geniusness of nature cure in their life.

Gandhiji recorded in his autobiography that he had a great desire to become a doctor and serve the people. But his strict Vaisnava family background never permitted him to do. Latter on, when he was in England he conducted number of experiments in diet. He was a vegetarian by birth. When he prepared his journey to England, he gave three vows to his mother which are connected with religion, morals and diet. He followed these vows in England. There he became a strict vegetarian and found a society of vegetarians. He was the secretary of the vegetarian society.

Gandhiji conducted some experiments in nature cure in England. Later on, he conducted experiments in hydrotherapy, mudtherapy, suntherapy, etc. He condemned the allopathy system of medicine as immoral. The hospital, according to Gandhiji, is the institution of sin. He says that the quakes are better than the professional allopathic doctors.

Gandhiji put nature cure as alternative to allopathic system of medicine. In nature cure human health is more important than the disease. In allopathy disease gets important place. Nature cure needs no costly medicine, apparatus and huge buildings. In Nature cure what is emphasised is a hygienic way of life, diet control, meditation, living with the nature, etc. With a little knowledge about diet, function of the body, structure of the body, disease treatment, everybody can treat their disease and live a happy life.

The Constructive Programmes in general and the nature cure in particular was neglected by the politicians who came to power. This is due to the lack of vision about the future of the nation and mankind. The professionalism is flowing in all the fields which includes medicines also. The huge hospitals, pharmaceutical companies and highly specialised doctors are not be proved about but the symbols which each and every rational being must be ashamed of. Disease is a punishment given by nature for wrong way of life, what is needed is complete rest and change towards the natural life.

Natural resources are available in plenty in India. The nature-cure needs morality, spirituality and disciplines. All our physical, mental and spiritual disorders are due to indiscipline. If the disorderliness was set right diseases will disappear from man. Gandhiji emphasised the following Do's and Don't in our life. If one follows a strict life according to one's own religious principles there is very little possibility for him to go to a physician. One can look after one's own health. One need not to be a slave to any medical or pharmaceutical professionals. According to Gandhiji, all kinds of slavery must be thrown away. One must not be slave to anybody directly or indirectly, knowingly or unknowingly. In the field of health the only real system which gives complete freedom and happiness to the individual is nature cure.

Man is the result of what he eats. The religion of Gandhiji directed him towards vegetarian diet. The simplicity in life once again pressed him to follow simple diet which is vegetarian. Apart from these there is also the economic reasons.

One of the drawbacks of the modern allopathic system is, that, it is unethical. It never respect the life principles. One's own religious sentiment and feeling is killed by the following of the allopathic medicine. For the sake of experiments, thousands of small beings are being killed without any reverence for life.

During 1942-44 when Gandhiji was in Aga Khan Palace, he wrote a small pamphlet on key to the Health in Gujarati. Dr. Susila Nair translated this book into English. In the preface of his book Gandhiji says, 'Anyone who observes the rules of health mentioned in the book will find that he got it a real key to unlock the gates leading him to health. He will not need to knock at the doors of doctors'.

In key to health, it is narrated that tea, coffee, tobacco and alcohol are unwanted things for a sane individual. Health is the real wealth. Human beings spend a lot of money in order to keep themselves in a healthy conditions. Especially in India, both Government and individuals spend a lot of money for health. The hospitals are increasing day to day. Gandhiji as a futurologists realised this danger and prescribed naturopathy as alternative medical system.

Both individual and society need a vision about their future. The past history reveals our mistakes and help us to plan for a better future. Gandhiji in his life learned the high values of naturopathy by his own experience. He suffered with so many diseases. He cured himself by diet control and other nature-cure methods like mud-bath, sun-bath, exercise, etc. He conducted experiments upon his friends and family members in order to find out the validity of nature cure. He read so many books on nature cure. He moved with the followers of nature cure.

All the principles of nature cure direct man towards a disciplined life. Man's life is different from that of the animals because he is living with the sense of rationality. He is not only gifted with analytical power but also synthetical. The nature-cure system is based upon the findings of the great medical men who are considered to be the highest rank doctors in allopathy. For instance, Hippocrates is considered as the father of medicine. If one anlyses Hippocrate's method, it is purely a naturopathic method. The nature-cure system has a philosophy of its own which is lacking in the modern method of medicines. In India, all the nature-cure rules and regulations centre is nothing but living in a natural surroundings in the midst of mountains, valleys or seashores. Fasting is recommended in all religions. In naturopathy fasting is the best medicine. The diet control is recommended by the naturopathy experts.

Nature cure is really a way of disciplined life and not a treatment. It begins with the treatment but leads the individual towards a higher way of life in which he lives cooperatively with all that exists and within himself he lives in perfect harmony. Both internal and external peace is the highest ideal which nature cure gives.

Thinkers such as Ivan Illich, Shelton writes books on the need for natural way of life. The yogatheraphy, massage treatment, diet control, etc., are now international. Even in Russia people are treated in nature cure hospitals. The sportsmen are trained in yoga for improving the skills.

Bhoodan

Gandhiji's idea of trusteeship, was translated into action by his disciple Vinoba Bhave. He gave life to the concept by introducing the Bhoodan and Gramdan movement. Gandhiji has considered Vinoba as his spiritual heir. The task of translating the Sarvodaya philosophy into a plan of action was taken by Vinoba in a shape of Bhoodan movement, which took the shape of Gramdan and Sampatidan.

Bhoodan Movement

The Bhoodan movement was started by Vinoba on April 15, 1951 in the Telangana region of Andhra Pradesh. The reason for starting this movement was a violent struggle between the landlords and the landless for land. Under the guidance of Vinoba, Akhil Bharathiya Sarva Seva Sangh took up the challenge to translate into reality the objectives of the Sarvodaya Philosophy. The basic objective of Bhoodan has been to inspire the people to develop a selfless attitude and feelings for the good of the masses. According to Gandhiji, "What Bhoodan says about land is true of all our possessions, including even knowledge and skill. All wealth is a social product and no earning is possible without social cooperation. Whatever we possess, therefore, belongs to the society. We are no more than trustees of what we have, implicitly charged by the society to take good care of our own trust and use it for the benefit not of ourselves but of all our fellow men". The concept of Bhoodan is based on the principle of a partyless democracy. To quote Vinoba, ". . . in a sense 'Bhoodan' is itself an intensely and deeply political movement. A movement that aims so utterly to revolutionise man and society cannot be but political. But it is politics of the kind I have described above – not the politics of parties, elections, parliaments and governments; but politics of the people – not 'Rajniti' but 'Lokniti'. It does not aim merely at getting land from the people and distributing it among the landless. It tries to abolish the gap between the haves and have-nots through non-violent means of *Satya* and *Ahimsa*." Love and cooperation should be the basic principles governing the individual and social behaviour. Social justice and equality should be the main objectives. "First of all, we must realize that 'Bhoodan' is not a programme of merely collecting and distributing land. It is rather the first step towards total revolution – social, political and economic. It stands for a society which would strive for the good of all, and in which everybody would be happy. In such a society there should be no distinction of high and low. Justice and Equality would form its distinguishing features and exploitation in any form would be completely eliminated. Power and authority would vest with the people in the true sense, they would regulate and administer their own affairs. Central authority would be sought to be extinguished, and if it is continued to exist, the sphere and extent of its operations would be minimized. The village will have all the authority and jurisdiction required."

The Bhoodan believes in universal brotherhood, which starts from the lowest level. Starting from the individual it extends to the village, the nation and, ultimately the whole world. "Bhoodan is thus a great mass movement of conversion and the creation of a new climate of thought and value of life. It brings about a living and immediate revolution in the minds of men and their mutual relationship. It attacks and corrects here and now the system of exploitation and inequality. It teaches men to share what they have with their fellowmen". *Dan* does not imply charity because the feelings of charity is against the spirit of equality and brotherhood. ". . . Bhoodan is not a charity movement, that behind it is Mahatma Gandhi's theory of trusteeship, in other words, the simple yet potent truth that man is not the master of what he possesses but only a trustee of what in reality belongs to the society."

In 1951, the Third Anniversary of Sarvodaya Conference of Constructive Workers was held in Hyderabad. Vinoba preferred to cover the three hundred miles from Wardha to Hyderabad on foot. This was mainly not to save the time but to get more acquaintance with people, their problems and to solve the same from a non-violent angle. Reaching Hyderabad for the conference, Vinoba was fully prepared for confronting the challenges ahead. On the last day of the Conference, i.e., 11th April, 1951 he expressed the desire to tour the communist-infested area of Telangana district chiefly for the purpose of propagating the message of peace and harmony. He wanted to study the facts at first hand, before returning to Wardha. "What would happen during this sojourn or thereafter was known only to God", remarked Vinoba, leaving Shivrampalli he reached Hyderabad and took the opportunity of meeting some communists in jail and he had a very frank and cordial talk with them. He visited the village of Pochampalli comprising of 90 families. He rested for a while in the village school building, got up suddenly and walked and started his round with the Harijan colony and entered several cottages to see their plight with his own eyes. The Harijans surrounded him and entreated: "We are very poor, we are also unemployed and therefore unhappy. Please help us".

"In what way can I help You? enquired Vinoba.

"We want only work and nothing else. Please give us some land, so that we may work hard on it to eke out our livelihood".

Vinoba, not knowing what to do, asked them, "How much land do you really require?"

After conferring among themselves for a while, one of them said: "Only 80 acres will do. We are 40 families, and two acres for each family will be quite adequate for our purpose". In this way the landless people in that village approached him and asked for his help in getting land for cultivation for their sustenance. Vinoba began to think seriously about this matter, but no solution was in sight. He, therefore quietly said, "I will find out from the Government whether it is possible to allot any land to you. This is a difficult question. Even so, I will try to explore the possibilities." And then, it suddenly struck him that someone in the village audience in the evening prayer meeting may like to donate some land for these poor Harijans. He lifted his eyes at the gathering, and remarked rather casually, "Brothers, is there anybody amongst you who can help these Harijan Friends?" Surprisingly, one Mr. Ramachandra Reddy came forward to donate 100 acres of land. Ramachandra Reddy stood up, looked at Vinoba with folded hands and said "Please do accept my donation of 100 acres". Neither Vinoba nor the members of his party could believe these words. But Ramachandra Reddy continued standing with his hands folded and awaiting Vinoba's concurrence. Vinoba was over-whelmed with emotion. It was, really a miracle. The Harijans asked for only 80 acres, and the donor spontaneously offered 100 acres. After wiping the tears with his upper cloth, Vinoba said, "I have come here with empty hands and will proceed to the next village tomorrow morning again with empty hands. Both the donor and the donee are present here in our midst. Let them exchange the land in our presence. The donor should also help the Harijan friends with some money and implements for cultivating the land in cooperative way". Ramachandra Reddy gently bowed before Vinoba and accepted the responsibility. The Harijans also touched his feet with joy and satisfaction. Vinoba had no words to thank the donor. Apart from evoking an immediate response for solving problems presented to him, it also gave birth to a highly revolutionary strategy based on peaceful co-existence, i.e., Bhoodan movement.

The following excerpts from Vinoba, highlight his imagination and future plan for solving the land problem in India. "That night when I went to bed I could not sleep. I was thinking over the event. What has happened to me today? I am a mathematician, I began to work but how much land would be needed for all the landless people in India. I came to the conclusion that fifty crore, fifty million acres, will be required for distribution, that is one-sixth of all cultivable land in India. I could not believe that people would offer that amount of land. The idea had come to me and attacked me and my mind tried to resist because I was not ready to accept. And so I hesitated. But a voice from within myself told me that if I doubt, I do not put my faith in the power of love and God, then I must abandon my belief in non-violence and follow the violent way of communists. You can't sit quiet any longer. You must either go this way or that way. God puts the hunger into the child's belly and he also puts the milk into the mother's breast; so if you go begging in the name of God, you will get a response".

"But I had only a hundred acres of land in my hand, and this was a question of asking for fifty million acres. I did not consult any of my friends or any institution because they would have said that I may expect to get thousands of acres, but I could not expect to get million – so I decided to go ahead, by myself, to start begging for land and to see how people respond".

"The next day in the morning I started for the next village. The village people had prepared breakfast for me. I told them that I won't breakfast, I won't break my fast while my country-men are hungry; give me a few acres of land for my breakfast. And God's will was there and they gave me twenty-five acres".

This was the birth of the great Bhoodan movement. The sudden miracle at Pochampalli village thrilled his whole being and Vinoba clearly recognised the hand of God in this unforeseen event. Addressing the village gathering after prayers, he remarked, "Man does not act merely on the strength of his own thinking. There is always a divine hand behind such noble thinking. There is always a divine hand behind such noble actions. I am a man of faith, and work for me. I will walk from village to village to seek land donations for the poor". He toured on foot asking for land donations.

Gradually the message of the peaceful and non-violent revolution spread into other parts of the country and it gained momentum in course of time in various states. *Padayatras* were organized for propagating the message and collecting the lands to be distributed to the landless. Vinoba was fully convinced that if this scheme is implemented on a nation-wide scale, there would be no land problem as there would be enough land for distribution among the landless poor.

In every village, land donations poured in, and Vinoba was convinced that God wanted him to continue this movement tirelessly with faith and resolution. The historic Telangana tour lasted for 51 days and Vinoba passed through some 200 villages and received 12,200 acres of land for distribution among the landless. Not a single village refused to give the gifts, the average being 240 acres a day. Even after Vinoba left Telangana, the local workers were able to collect a further 1,00,000 acres as a result of the tempo created by the Bhoodan missions. Returning from Telangana, Vinoba reached Paramdhan Ashram on 26th June 1951, and he received an invitation from the Prime Minister, to advise the Planning Commission at Delhi. He decided to start for Delhi on foot. He also wanted to test the Bhoodan idea in areas, which were not haunted by Communists. During the first week of this *Padayatra*, he covered about 110 miles and obtained 2000 acres of land, an average of little less than 300 acres per day.

The State governments passed Bhoodan Yagna Acts. The State Boards were created to look after the Bhoodan and redistribution. The allottees who received the Bhoodan lands should cultivate them within three years, otherwise the Bhoodan Boards would take away those lands. Though the allottees would have the full rights of enjoyment and rights of inheritance, they cannot sell, mortgage or lease them out.

Even when statutory efforts were being made, Vinoba was adamant that he would accept only what is given with love. He did not consider the scheme as a success, if lands were given unwillingly by big landowners. In the second phase, therefore, he approached the middle class landowners and explained the purpose of Bhoodan and prospects it can bring in. He appealed to them with examples quoted from the epics such as Sudama's small gifts of rice to Lord Krishna. He was certain that all have the capacity to give a small portion which will produce the desired effect in helping the landless. He was more keen to bring in change among the landlords than on the stress laid on the number of acres they donate. He was happy that "everyone's heart is changing" and observes that "if all hearts can change in this manner, legislation will not be necessary. The whole problem can be solved with love".

Vinoba's main task was to propagate the notion that all wealth including the lands belong to everyone. He expected the constructive workers to act as catalysts in society so as to bring in a meaningful social revolution. Bhoodan is an all-embracing revolution that seeks to bring about an over all transformation of human values and thus establishes a new order wherein the individual interest will exist only as a part of the wider social interest. In 1958, Vinoba had kept the target of collecting 50 million acres of land. He could reach to a level of 4.2 million acres and this could achieve a partial success of 8.4 per cent. However, it should not be analysed from a quantitative view, but the qualitative change that was brought is more meaningful and long lasting. Compared to the Governmental efforts, through legislation which yielded only 2.2 million acres of land, Vinoba's efforts proved to be a better success.

The Bhoodan movement has been weak on the publicity front. There are not many journals and books on the subject. Adequate information is not available about the development work done by Bhoodan lands. Lack of facts and figures in detail regarding development work done in this sphere makes it difficult to present an overall assessment. Bhoodan is a mass movement and that people themselves should organise it, the samities were dissolved. So, the Bhoodan movement has not been able to catch the imagination of the masses it was expected of it. The slow moving legislative machinery should be geared up. The farmers who had donated the land were forced to pay the revenue for land given away by them because of the time consuming process involved in making the transfer legal. This enable the donors taking back the land from tenants earlier given by them in the Bhoodan. The small size of holding distributed to the landless with improper and insufficient facilities for even àn ordinary utilization forced them to abandon the land so received in the Bhoodan movement. Another factor which can contribute to the success of the movement is the help from the government. The government can help the movement by providing persons capable of carrying out development activities. It can provide the needed trained technical personnel to carry out the projects. Government aid is desirable for the successful implementation of the Bhoodan plans. But then the Government should have no power to interfere with the working of the movement.

Suggestions Regarding the Working of Bhoodan Movement

1. No donation of land should ordinarily be accepted from those villagers who have holding of less than five acres.
2. Inferior land should be avoided as far as possible.
3. No uncultivable land received in donation should be brought under cultivation.

4. The organisers of the movement should provide necessary inputs and equipment to the landless peasants.
5. Full and detailed records of the donation of the land, livestock and material should be kept. The Sarva Seva Sangh should see that the records are properly maintained.
6. The Government should be urged to take up the necessary legislation for just and equitable distribution or redistribution of land, cattle and other material among landless.

The Bhoodan movement has been successful in bringing about some change in the people's attitude but other results of its working have not been very spectacular. The remarkable success of the Bhoodan movement can be judged from the fact that it has been developed into the Gramdan movement. In 1961 Vinoba said, "The little achievement we have made so far is not at all negligible". Dr. Rajendra Prashad highly appreciated the event of Bhoodan as a spirit that "gives a vision of the social order that Mahatma Gandhi envisaged and kindles and enlivens the hope of its attainment". Dr. Radhakrishnan commented it as 'an act of faith that would bring a unity of mind, thought and purpose in India'.

Criticism about Bhoodan Movement

1. Absence of clarity regarding the objective of the Movement.
2. Lop-sided approach to the agrarian problem. It aims to help and provide land only to the landless villagers.
3. The movement provides insufficient land to the landless.
4. It leads to the division and fragmentation of already small and scattered fields.
5. Bhoodan creates uneconomic holdings. As poor person join the movement by donating a small piece of land from their already tiny plots, the holdings are reduced to uneconomic units.
6. Most of the land donated is of inferior quality and some of it is extremely poor.
7. It will hardly be successful in rehabilitating all the landless agricultural labourers.
8. The slogan 'land to the landless' seems to emphasise the indispensable character of land for those who do not have it.
9. Bhoodan stands in the way of mechanised farming. The small five acres holdings that the Bhoodan aims at providing to the

landless of the country are unsuitable for mechanised farming.

10. Its machinery is not efficient and the distribution process is very slow.
11. The target for land-gift was set at fifty million acres which was to be achieved by the end of 1957. It was too high an ambition for voluntary movement depending entirely on moral persuasion. Up to the end of 1957, only 1/10th of the target fixed has been achieved.
12. It was claimed by the protagonists of Bhoodan that they were not enamored of collectivisation and they intended rather to give land to the millions of landless labourers in the countryside on an individual or family basis to begin with.

Gramdan

Bhoodan was followed by Gramdan. Gramdan, literally means 'village gift' whereas Bhoodan means 'land gift'. The Bhoodan movement gave birth to Gramdan. The Gramdan was first put into operation in September 1952, in a village named Mangroth in Uttar Pradesh. Under the Gramdan, the resources of the village are to be exploited equally by each and every member of the village community. The entire village community works for its prosperity and welfare. "I will believe that as people join Gramdan and gather some strength, corruption will come to an end. I do not say that no corruption ever took place in the Gramdan village or the government officials, overseers, etc., did not accept illegal amounts in Gramdan villages. But if you compare them with other villages, there is a world of differences. This is why there is some hitch over Gramdan from their side". For social and economic progress, the gramdan movement is at the top of all other programmes. "The changes that can be brought about even in the initial stages by Gramdan are of such a vital character as cannot be obtained by any amount of official work, or programmes of political parties, or activities of Panchayat Raj or Community Development or Five-year Plans. . . . All these programmes will never be able to match, in quality or quantity, the attainments of Gramdan".

Vinoba entered the village Mangroth and this proved to be a red letter day in the annals of Bhoodan Movement. The residents of the village presented him with 101 acres of land. Vinoba accepted the gift and repeated – "all land belongs to God". With this message in their hearts, they returned home to consider his appeal. Diwan Shatrughan

Singh was a devoted constructive worker. In the post-prayer meeting at Mangroth, he announced his decision to donate whole of his land to Bhoodan. The villagers also agreed to join the movement. Mangroth, thus earned the distinction of being the first Gramdan village. The total number of families in that village was 107. After the declaration of Gramdan, the land belonged to the village and all the families decided to work with their hands and jointly enjoyed the fruits of cultivation. The planning of the crops was to be decided by the village panchayat in order to achieve self-sufficiency in food-grains and vegetables.

To quote Jayaprakash Narayan, "In the beautiful revolution of Gramdan, ownership was not abolished by force of any kind, but freely surrendered to the community". G. Ramachandran says, "Gramdan means a large fund of unity of mind in the village, a readiness to face practical changes in the social and economic structure of village, the courage to walk on the new road and readiness on the part of the individual to make a sacrifice in favour of the community, and therefore, something precise, unambiguous and challenging in the confused situation affecting the rural areas today. . . . Gramdan is a mental and economic revolution representing the re-assertion of modern world. Gramdan is a complete breakaway from the tradition of private ownership of land which has been the rock upon which the life of the village in India has rested during uncounted centuries. And yet, the entire spirit underlying Gramdan is in harmony with the spirit of the culture of India which has always put renunciation for above power".

According to Prof. D.R. Gadgil, the Gramdan movement "is an unprecedental movement with many and complex implications and very great potentialities". Louis Fischer has described it as "the most creative thought coming out of the East". Shriman Narayan says, "It is revolutionising the basic values of life and the method for achieving the objective is through non-violence, democracy and conversion of hearts in place of class war, hatred and violence. Moreover the Bhoodan and the Gramdan movements are able to touch the most backward and poorest sections of the population. It is being realised on all hands that our development schemes have not been able so far to ameliorate the economic condition of the lowest sections of our people. . . . The co-operating way in Gram Raj is able to touch the felt needs of the poorest sections in an effective manner. It is from this point of view that the Gramdan movement deserves utmost encouragement".

Gramdan provides opportunity to eradicate the class distinctions of have and have-nots but creates a sense of service and sacrifices among the people. Gramdan provides a method of land distribution by weeding out private ownership of land and giving the land to everyone in the village at a ratio of the requirements of each family based on the number of its members. That every man in the village should receive a plot of land to work upon, is the fundamental idea of Gramdan. This is to be achieved by doing away with the unequal distribution of land and by avoiding uneconomic holdings of and unduly large holdings of land. The method of land distribution may differ from village to village and each village can adopt its own course. All the land of the village can be pooled into one common plot and distributed to each family for cultivation according to their need and strength to work. Every individual will cease to be the owner of land and the right of ownership will vest in the village community as a whole. The concept of Gramdan is a comprehensive one as it envisages to solve so many problems at one and at the same time.

Examples

1. The problem of abolition of intermediaries no longer remains in a gramdan village.
2. The problem of landless labourers is automatically solved.
3. The problem of land ceiling does not arise at all in a village after gramdan.
4. The problem of cooperative or collective farming to which gramdan movement is a practical approach, is solved to a considerable extent.
5. It does away with uneconomic holdings and reduces the undue pressure of population on small plots of land.
6. It incidentally does away with the sub-division and fragmentation of holdings.

Explaining the significance of Gramdan, Vinoba points out five-fold programme of this revolution:

1. Creating an atmosphere of economic equality and liberty.
2. Reviving the cultural life of the society by making the village a family.
3. Discarding the land ownership concept, thus creating ethical

atmosphere to settle disputes mutually without litigation, bad blood or bitterness.
4. Establishing old *Varnashrama Dharma* which is derivative of peace, fearlessness, compassion and faith.
5. Protecting the society from outward aggression thus acting as a defence measure.

The salient feature of a Gramdan Village can best be summarised as follows:

1. Involvement of more people enthusiastically to work for its aims so as to make them proud of their own village.
2. Besides agriculture preference to village crafts is helpful in reducing the burden of population on land.
3. Agricultural production, to begin with, may take the form of owner-cultivation or cooperative farming but the ideal to be striven is that of the village communal farming or Gramdan farming in which the whole village will work as a joint family.
4. The multi-craft and many-sided sarvodaya method of production ensures that each village and each family will have to devote itself not only to agriculture but one or more crafts.

Explaining the significance of Gramdan, Vinoba enumerated seven basic objectives.

1. Elimination of poverty.
2. Awakening the feelings of affection and love in the hearts of the land-owners; thus improving the moral atmosphere in the country;
3. Strengthening the society by forging bonds of mutual help and fellow-feelings, thus avoiding what is as a rule witnessed elsewhere in the form of class hatred between the land-holders on one side and landless on the other;
4. Revival and furtherance of Indian culture based on our unique philosophy of *Yajna, Dana* and *Tapa*, thus strengthening the faith of man in true religion.
5. Building a new social order on the basis of voluntary bodily labour, non-possession, co-operation and self-reliance;
6. Giving an opportunity to all the political parties in the country to come together on a common platform and work unitedly, thus

rooting out bitterness and self-agrandisement; and

7. Helping world peace.

Gramdan has transformed the land gift movement into village gift. Certain conditions, are to be fulfilled so as to be called as Gramdan village. They are as follows:

1. More than 50 per cent of the total land should be donated by private land owners.
2. Atleast two/thirds of the adult residents should join the movement.
3. Disputes should not be taken to the police or to the court, but should be settled in the village itself by the special committee set up for the purpose.
4. The members of the village should contribute a portion of their income as *Gram Kosh* (Community Fund) say 1/40 of their agricultural produce for the welfare of the community, with first priority to the weaker sections of the community.
5. There should be a duly constituted Gram Sabha and all adults residing in the village should be eligible for membership.
6. Individual owners should be willing to transfer their ownership to the Gram Sabha and should allow a minimum of 5 per cent of their lands to be distributed among the landless in the village.

It is an admitted fact that Bhoodan and Gramdan did not meet with complete success. However, Vinoba could effect a change in attitude, which would by itself lead to socio-economic impact. In 1957, he wrote, "let it be understood clearly that increasing agricultural production is certainly not the aim and object of Bhoodan and Gramdan. That would be only incidental. Its main objects is to widen man's loyalty to the entire society". Again he says, "I am not really worried about how the work of reconstruction will proceed in the Gramdan villages. The task of building up a new society of the free and equal in the Gramdan villages is a responsibility which all have to share. It is not our private or personal commitment. I am out to pose problems, not to solve them. I am not a full-stop; I voluntarily give up their private ownership is my task".

Regarding the attitudinal change, both Bhoodan and Gramdan envisaged and effected a high degree of result. The movement directly influences the life of the landlords and landless people. By adopting

Gandhian ideas, Vinoba could keep the social reconstruction more alive at a period when even the educated people were labelling the Gandhian concepts as irrelevant. It induced interest in the individual to dwell into Gandhian thought and reassess its relevance.

Weakness

The Bhoodan and Gramdan movements are not without defects. Too much reliance on the mechanism organisation, lack of faith in land donors, lack of committed Sarvodaya workers, too much of focus on some selected areas etc., have resulted in an imbalanced percolation of the ideology and an uneven spread-up of the message contained in it. More rigid approach to the target-oriented policy led to many lacunae and lack of acceptance of the scheme widely. The failure in devising some short-term strategies for the solution of the pressing problems of landless was another defect. Further it failed to influence the Government effectively. Thus the spirit of the movement gradually got diluted.

As of now, only 30 per cent of the land have been redistributed. The reason for this are: (1) The land donation should be made legal. It is a difficult, tedious and complex phenomenon and takes much time and energy. The disputes of ownership, the donations by exrulers, etc., have caused the delay; (2) Though the landlords have made the donations, the intermediary agents have refused to vacate the donated lands. (3) Some landlords after donating the land on the eve of nationwide movement, have tried to withdraw the donation after a second thought. (4) A major part of the lands were barren, rocky, undulating, eroded, swampy or otherwise degraded, being unfit for redistribution. (5) The Sarvodaya movement lacked resources, manpower and dynamism. The old guards prevented the youths from entering the movement. (6) The Bhoodan Boards have acute shortage of financial and human resources.

Up to July 1971, 1,68,058 villages have been donated to the movement. This movement has shown that the masses can generate a new sense of self-help and self-reliance among themselves by voluntary pooling their land and capital resources for the good of the community. Gramdan villages have their own administrative set up. The Gramdan sabha prepares a production plan for the village as a whole on an equitable and scientific basis.

Shanti Sena

The race for a material progress has thwarted the prevalence and progress of peace in the world. Every nation is rapidly striving to accumulate, as much as possible, arms and weapons, with the result the world is facing an insecure future. Consequently, the life is, day by day becoming less happy. As we are aware the world has still not fully recovered from the setback caused by a 'baby bomb' that was dropped in Hiroshima on 6th August 1945.

There are various measures adopted to re-establish 'peace' on the Earth. But it is conveniently forgotten that true peace can inhere in minds that are free from the tussels of life and seriously contrasting social set-up. The human nature has moved in the direction of simple to complex and it has now to march backward to simplicity to attain the true peace in human life.

As a devoted votary of non-violence and peace, Gandhiji gave much thought to the establishment of peace. He offered the concept of Peace Brigade (Shanti Sena) in this connection. Many could not understand or appreciate the concept and its developmental values.

The Concept

By establishment of Shanti Sena, Gandhiji desired to organise a non-violent force to intervene in the conflicting situation, to root out the causes of violence and peacelessness and to establish a society dominated by peace, characterised by truth and non-violence. He considered it as a progressive means to build up a Sarvodaya society. In the words of Vinoba, "Shanti Sena will not merely go into action when disturbances take place; on the contrary, it will be at work all time. Because of this, it cannot be separated in thought from the whole idea of Sarvodaya". Thus the idea of Shanti Sena has not only a conflict resolving purpose but also it works as constructive force for the all-round development of the society.

Aims of Shanti Sena

The objective of Peace Brigade was to lay the foundation of a society committed for welfare and development of the people. Such a society has to be firmly founded on truth and non-violence. In his own words, Gandhi says, "Shanti Sena acts unlike armed men, as well in times of peace disturbances. They would be constantly engaged in the duty of seeking occasions for bringing warring communities together carrying on peace propaganda engaging in activities that would bring and keep them in touch with every single person, male and female, adult and child, in the perish or division". Thus, Shanti Sena has a developmental and preventive value embodied within it.

History

The unending communal riots made Gandhi to think in terms of need for establishing a 'Peace Brigade'. He not only gave shape to the concept, but tried to test the validity of the same. On 18th March, 1938, he enunciated the concept of Shanti Sena through Harijan. As a follower of Gandhian ideology, Vinoba realises the importance of Shanti Sena. During his southern tour, he established the first unit of Shanti Sena on 27th August, 1957. Gradually the concept and message of Shanti Sena spread over to various parts of the country. Subsequently, many peace centres were established. Jayaprakash Narayan held the Chairmanship of All India Shanti Sena Mandal for long time. In course of time the Gandhigram Rural University in Anna District of Tamil Nadu, played a key role in promoting the concept and practice of peace Brigade under the guidance of Dr. M. Aram, the then Vice-Chancellor.

Qualifications of Shanti Sena

For becoming a peace soldier certain qualifications were prescribed. They are as under:

(a) An unrelenting faith in non-violence and in the supremacy of moral law;
(b) fearlessness and freedom from retaliatory attitude;
(c) tolerance to all religions (*Sarvadharma Samabhava*);
(d) Unreproaching character and strict impartiality;
(e) positive contact and effective relationship with the local people;
(f) selflessness and non-partisanship;
(g) indiscriminatory attitude and faith in quality;
(h) modesty, cleanliness and gentleness;
(i) non-possessive attitude and faith in simplicity;
(j) trust in one another and freedom from hatred and enmity;

(k) partylessness;
(l) discipline;
(m) love for social service;
(n) interest in national integration; and
(o) faith in the dignity of labour.

Structure of Shanti Sena

The outline of the structure of Shanti Sena is also specified. The membership should not be very large, that is, the size of the non-violent corps will be small yet efficient. The members should contact with the local people and establish good rapport with them. As the members hail from the same locality, their relation with the society is cordial and intimate. Membership should not be based on physical fitness, but should be based on character. They may wear badges for identity, preferably of yellow colour and should be in white uniform. They should not carry weapons but should have the knowhow of First-aid and fire-fighting. A peace soldier should cultivate the art of silence. They should be trained for practising *Brahmacharya*.

Functions of Shanti Sena

Functionally, Shanti Sena has two aspects – 'Seva' and 'Shanti'. In Vinoba's view, "the Peace Army will be primarily one of service, it will be also a service army and only on occasion of violence, it will do the work of Shanti Sena. The Seva Sena will provide the Shanti Sena which can be used when there is an outbreak of violence". Vinoba further states, "Shanti Sena will help the poor, it will draw the attention of the rich to the sufferings of the poor, and with their sympathy, it will try to get rid of individual land ownership. It will give personal service to sick. It will try to increase productivity in the village. It will arrange for education. There will be no dissension in the village if the Shanti Sena serves it in these ways. It will be the Shanti Sena task to destroy the root cause of unrest – the gulf between the haves and have-nots, cruelty, the pride of ownership, the insistence on mine and thine, on high and low, on caste distinctions, on religious differences and disputes."

It is neither the duty nor is it possible for a Peace Soldier to find a solution for all problems. He has to resist in times of riots and violence. Functionally they can substitute the police. If there are previous warnings of storm, they could prepare themselves to deal with the situation. Some times, the full-time workers are also suggested. At other times, the workers should have sufficient leisure to serve the purpose. The maintenance of the Peace Brigade should be out of the funds collected by means of *Sampattidan* and *Sarvodaya Patram.* The number does not matter, but it is more of the spiritual and moral preparedness and sacrificial attitude that is more important. Devotional songs and Bhajan with the assistance of musical instruments can help such peace workers. Sufficient training schools should be established for preparing the peace workers. Refresher Programmes are also useful.

Women also have a crucial role to play in developing a strong unit of Shanti Sena. Vinoba says, "if women will take up the work of Shanti Sena, the face of the world will change and we shall be able to achieve freedom from the problems which we are facing today in the country and abroad. Man cannot do all this. They are not in their poor senses. They cannot think it out. The only solution they can find is to increase armaments. Thus, in this age of science, when men's brains have become paralysed, if our women came forward with their divine qualities of restraint and modesty and use their mother power, they can establish the rules of compassion".

It is necessary for a peace soldier to cultivate the social service outlook and be fully prepared to help the people in danger and distress. They should discipline the mind through spiritual and moral ways and should uphold the qualities of a true worker with firm faith in Truth and *Ahimsa.* Then only they can succeed in their task of serving the society for maintaining the peace.

From the inception of the concept, there has been steady effort to implement the Shanti Sena ideology. A concrete examples of a solid effort is that of Gandhigram Rural University – Shanti Sena unit with so much of practical work rendered for the society.

Lord Mountbatten's tributes to Gandhiji as 'one man boundary force' is not an exaggeration when we consider the living faith of Gandhiji in the power of Truth and non-violence. Vinoba called him as a Commander and Soldier of Peace Army. "As a commander he issued the order 'do or die' and as a soldier he obeyed it." Thus the life of Gandhiji fully reviews the true picture of Shanti Sainik.

On the day of 30th January 1948, when he fell down by the assassin's bullets, he was fully prepared to pardon the assassin. The unforgettable incident converted a tragedy into triumph. This incident had a high dramatic value for conveying the central theme of Peace Brigade as well.

3

GANDHIAN CONCEPTION OF MAN

The Divine Principle in Man

THE STUDY of human nature is the most interesting and the most beneficial of all studies. The more we study ourselves, the better we can understand the universe, its laws, and the truth that underlies its phenomena. It is said, 'man is the epitome of the universe; whatever exists in the world is to be found in the body of man'. That is, man is the microcosm of the macrocosm. On the one hand, man is filled with the tendencies and propensities which characterise the lower animals. But on the other, we see him manifesting through the actions of his life all those noble qualities that adorn the character of one, whom we honour, respect, and worship the Divine Being. Human nature seems to be the most wonderful blending of that which is animal with that which is called Divine. It is like the twilight before day-break, through which the darkness of the night of the animal passes into the glorious sunshine of the supreme wisdom. Human nature may be called the state of transition from the animal into the divine. The animal nature includes the love of self or the attachment of one's self to one's body and to everything related to the body and the senses, desire for sense pleasure and enjoyments, clinging to earthly life, fear of death and the struggle for existence. Each of these qualities or tendencies is to be found in the lower animals as well as in human beings, the difference being only in degrees and not in kind.

The savage man who lives such as a wild beast in a cave or under trees and does not know how to build a house or cultivate the ground, but who sustains life by depending entirely upon fruits, roots, wild berries, or upon the birds and beasts that he can trap, expresses in all the actions of his life nothing more than what we have described as animal tendencies and animal propensities. If the Darwinian theory be true, then we can easily explain why there should be so little difference between primitive man and his distant ancestor, the Chimpanzee, or some other member of the anthropoid species. When the same wild man become partially civilised by learning to cultivate the land, to raise food and cook it, to build houses and live in communities, be no longer manifests these animal tendencies in their simpler and more savage forms. He gradually adopts more artful methods to accomplish his purpose. For instance, the struggle for existence depends chiefly upon physical force among savage tribes as well as among animals, while among civilised people in civilised countries a similar result in the form of the survival of the fittest is obtained, not by the display of brute force, but by art, skill, diplomacy, policy, lying, strategy, and hypocrisy. These are the offensive and defensive weapons of the so-called civilised man.

All the vicious qualities and wicked deeds such as murder, theft, robbery, and other crimes which are found in civilised communities are nothing but the expression of the animal tendencies of man, working under the heavy pressure of the rigid laws of society, State and Government. They proceed from love of self and extreme attachment to the animal nature. Being guided by these lower tendencies, man becomes extremely selfish, and does not recognise the rights and comforts of his fellow beings. On the contrary, he does everything to satisfy the cravings of his body and senses at the expense of his neighbours. But the moment that his savage man, or the man who lives like a lower animal being is to see the rights of others, learns to love and care for his fellow beings in the same way that he loves his own dear self and cares for his belongings, from that time he rises a step higher than the absolutely animal plane; he becomes truly human and gradually manifests the other qualities and tendencies that accompany this fundamental moral principle – to love one's neighbour as one's self.

Upon this foundation has been built the whole structure of ethics among all nations. The virtuous qualities such as disinterested love for humanity, mercy, justice, kindness towards others, forgiveness, self-sacrifice, all these help the animal man to expand his love of self and to subdue all the proceeds from purely selfish attachment to his own body and senses. The higher we rise above the animal plane, the wider becomes the circle of self-love, and instead of being confined to the body and senses of the individual, it becomes general, covering themselves, not merely of dearest relatives and nearest friends, but of neighbours, countrymen and at last, of all humanity. Thus, the more universal our love of self becomes, the nearer we approach the

Divinity, because the divine principles is the universal Being, whose love flows equally towards all living creatures, as the sun shines equally upon the heads of the virtuous and wicked.

The Spiritual Training of the Will

Man has the intelligence and capacity to control the process of nature and society, and to use these to ensure human fulfilment everywhere. But his will in perverse; it seeks the ways of folly; it is his enemy; and it will remain his enemy so long as it is in thraldom to his animal nature and to the little ego centred in that nature. It has to be turned in the direction of his divine nature within; then alone his intelligence and will and feeling fuse into a new value to emerge as buddhi, wisdom.

Vedanta teaches that when we speak of man or woman as the image of God, we do not mean his or her physical form but we mean the individual ego or the soul. If the divine Being or God be this universal spirit, then His image cannot be the physical form of man; this does not convey any idea or meaning at all. The ego or the soul of each individual man or woman is the image of Divinity. This idea has been beautifully expressed in *Vedanta*: In the cave of the heart have entered the two, the one is the eternal, absolute, real, perfect, and self-effulgent such as the sun, and the other the individual ego or soul, is like its reflection, or shadow, or image. The one is such as the fountain-head of the blessed qualities and the infinite source of all divine powers while the other contains the partial reflection of those qualities and powers.

Thus according to *Vedanta*, every individual soul, whether it be more or less animal in its thoughts and actions, possesses the divine image and is no other than the image of the divine principle or Being. The divine Being is one and universal, but its reflections or images are many. As the image of the sun, falling upon the dull and unpolished surface of a piece of metal does not properly reflect the grandeur and power of that self-luminous body but appears dull and imperfect, so the divine image, falling upon the dull surface of the animal nature, cannot reflect all the blessed qualities, cannot manifest all the divine powers, but, on the contrary, appears animal in its tendencies and propensities. As the same image of the sun will shine forth brighter and more effulgent, when the surface of the metal is polished, so the individual soul will show its brighter and more effulgent aspect and will more fully reflect the divine qualities, when the heart which contains the image is polished and made free from the dirt of animal desire and animal tendencies; then and then alone, this same individual soul will begin to manifest all the blessed qualities such as justice, mercy, kindness and disinterested love for all humanity. These powers are latent in all individuals, but they will be expressed when the heart is purified.

The perfect manifestation of these divine powers depends entirely upon the removal of all obstructions like desire for earthly pleasure for the enjoyments and comforts of earthly life, attachment to the gross physical body and to the senses, which force the individual soul to remain on the animal plane. Yet, however animal the expression of nature of an ordinary man of the world may be, his soul is still the image of the Divinity which holds potentially in its bosom all divine powers and all blessed qualities. Nay, even the souls of lower animals are potentially divine, according to *Vedanta*. The evolution of nature is required to bring out these potential tendencies, powers, and qualities into their actual and real manifestations. Climbing the ladder of the evolution of nature, each individual soul or germ of life expresses its latent powers, first through the limitations of the animal nature as animal tendencies and animal desires and lastly, as spiritual powers by rising above all limitations, by transcending the boundaries of the various circles of animals, moral and spiritual nature and approaching the abode of the infinite divine principle. At that time the individual soul becomes absolutely free from the bondage of nature, enjoys the supreme Bliss which is divine, and manifests all the blessed qualities. In passing through these various stages and individual ego studies its own powers gains experience and realises all the powers that are lying dormant with the soul, says Swami Abhedananda.

The *Upanishads* boldly proclaim that spirituality is the prerogative of every individual. This *Atman* the divine, the immoral, is the self of every man and woman and child. It is the true nature of man. It is also the true nature of all animals, but animals cannot realise it. It is only man with his unique psycho-physical system, aided by the psycho-social environment created by himself in the course of his evolution, that has the capacity to realise the truth. Man is specially fitted for this great adventure. He has certain advantages, and when he starts using these advantages he is able to rise to the highest level of spiritual life. The *Upanishads* tell us that wealth and power are not the highest glory of man. The *Upanishads* do condemn man's pursuit of worldly wealth and power; they never condemn any values pursued by man. Only they say, 'There is something better and higher than this'. The *Upanishads* ever urge us to go on to the realisation of this something better within us.

Universal Man

The *Upanishads* summon man to constant struggle to gain the highest, the struggle to achieve the eternal, the permanent, the immortal imbedded in life and experience. Other races and other cultures have spoken of man as a dominator of external nature, as a creator of values in the context of man's collective life. In Greek thought, for example, we have the concept of promothean spirit, the power of the human spirit to overcome external obstacles and establish man's supremacy over the forces of nature and, if necessary, over the forces of other human beings as well. The great defect in this line of thought, when pursued by itself, is that it does not carry all humanity together. It is based on the concept man dominating everything external to himself; it does not stress the need to chasten and overcome the age which results from such domination of his external environment. Man dominating his environment is a valid concept, it is a form of human excellence. The West has carried it to the highest level of expression; and we in India stand in great need of education in this excellence on a nation-wide scale. But this is not the highest that man is capable of; Indian thought will not accord it the highest point in the scale of human excellence. That point involves the transcendence of the ego and the emergence of the universal within man. When man achieves supreme self-transcendence he finds that there is nobody to dominate. He finds that he is one with all, for he has realised the self in all.

Gandhiji's Conception of Man

Gandhiji inherited the ancient Indian tradition, but he did not accept the tradition blindly, what was characteristic of him was that he infused a new dynamic element into the traditional passive attitude of our people by utilising 'the new positive ideas of modern Indian by assimilating them in thought, living them in his life and giving them social and political shapes'.

Man and Brute

Gandhiji admitted man's animal ancestry. 'We were, perhaps, all originally brutes, I am prepared to believe that we have become men by a slow process of evolution from the brute'. Again, 'Man must choose either of the two courses, the upward or the downward, but as he has the brute in him, he will more easily choose the downward course than the upward, especially when the downward course is presented to him in the beautiful garb . . . the downward instinct is embodied in them'.

But Gandhiji would not admit that man's nature was all evil. He emphatically asserted, 'man's nature is not essentially evil. Brute nature has been known to yield to the influence of love. You must never despair of human nature'. And 'Human nature will only find itself when it fully realises that to be human it has to cease to be beastly or brutal. Though we have the human form, without the attainment of the virtue of non-violence we still share the qualities of our remote reputed ancestor'.

Gandhiji did not look upon man as a mere brute. He regarded man as, above all, the soul. He believed that 'the dignity of man require, obedience to a higher law – to the strength of the spirit'. What distinguishes man from the brute? He says, 'We were born with brute strength, but we were born in order to realise God who dwells in us. That indeed is the privilege of man and it distinguishes him from the brute creation'. So like all the seers of the *Upanishads*, Gandhiji believed in the ultimate goal of man or human birth i.e. self-realisation. The essential difference between man and brute, according to him, can rise superior to the passions that he owns in common with the brute and, therefore, superior to selfishness and violence, which belong to the brute-nature and not to the immortal spirit of man. Gandhiji understood that as being the fundamental conception of Hinduism.

Man and God

Gandhiji as a believer in 'absolute oneness of God, and therefore of humanity', affirmed: 'What though we have many bodies? We have but one soul'. 'I believe in the essential unity of man and for that matter of all that lives'.

Gandhiji subscribed to the theological belief that, 'all life in its essence is one, and that the humans are working consciously or unconsciously towards the realisation of that identity'. 'Our existence as embodied beings is purely momentary; what are a hundred years in eternity? But if we shatter the chains of egotism, and melt into the ocean of humanity, we share the dignity. To feel that we are something is to set up a barrier between God and ourselves; to cease feeling that we are something is to become one with God'.

Gandhiji repeatedly said that it was more natural for man to be good than to be evil, though apparently, descent might seem easier than ascent. He believed that 'the divine powers within us are infinite'. Because of this divine element in man it was his firm belief that man is by nature going higher. He spoke of man as the part of God or of the Divine power. He looked upon every man as the incarnation of God. He was fond of quoting the Mohammedan saying: Man is not God; but neither is he different from the light of God. Dr. D.M. Metha after noting this fond citation of Gandhiji observes: 'Here again we find his preference for some type of identity — indifference relation which is differently maintained by the Vaishnava Vedantists and in recent times by Tagore. The Shankarites are advocates of rigid identity. Gandhiji tries to keep his conception of man and God mobile and dynamic by thinking of God as force, as life etc., as if to make him admit divergent lines of a manifestation, incarnation and inspiration.

The Oneness of Man

Gandhiji believed in the absolute oneness of God and therefore also of humanity. 'What though we have many bodies? We have but one soul. The rays of the sun are many through refraction. But they have the same source'. His belief in 'the essential unity of God and man and for that matter all that lives' has been stated by one commentator as being similar to the stoic idea of the universe as a divine whole and of mankind as an essential unity in which the individual could realise himself.

Gandhiji subscribed to the theological belief that all life in its essence is one, and that the humans are working consciously or unconsciously towards the realisation of that identity. In a mood of philosophic exaltation he could exclaim: 'Our existence as embodied beings is purely momentary; what are a hundred years in eternity? But if we shatter the charms of egotism and melt into the ocean of humanity we share its dignity. To feel that we are something is to set up barrier between God and ourselves; to cease feeling that we are something is to become one with God'.

About soul, Gandhiji said, 'Soul is apart from life. The latter is conditioned by the body, the former is not'. 'The soul is God head within man; it is self acting; it persists even after death; its existence does not depend upon the physical body; it is matter rarefied to the utmost limit. Hence whatever happens to one body, must affect the whole of the matter and the whole of spirit'. He held that belief that if one man gains spiritually, the whole world gains with him and if one man falls, the whole world falls to that extent'.

Man and Environment

Gandhiji, while admitting that man actually lived by habit, laid stress on the exercise of will. He said, 'while admitting that man actually lives by habit, I hold that it is better for him to live by the exercise of the will'. Self-direction involved for Gandhiji passing judgements on one's behaviour, justifying or condemning it. He recognised that in spite of the greatest effort for being detached, no man can altogether undo the effects of his environment or his upbringing. But he did not consider man to be merely a creature of circumstances'. It is man's privilege to overcome adverse circumstances'. One could see from Gandhiji's own life how he had been overcoming all the adverse circumstances coming in the way in his life to emerge a near-perfect man he was.

Self-restraint, Gandhiji, believed, was a positive factor in man's life for overcoming the adverse circumstances. In his autobiography, 'The brute by nature knows no self-restraint. Man is man because he is capable of, and only in so far as he exercises self-restraint'. Self-restraint implies control of the baser tendencies such as hatred and selfishness, and informing life with goodwill and love.

Gandhiji recognised the influence of environment on a man's character and that was why he was for changing the environment as it was given. 'It is because the rulers, if they are bad, are so, not necessarily or wholly by reason of birth, but largely because of their environment, that have hopes of their altering by their course . . . . If they are dominated by their environment, they do not surely deserve to be killed, but should be changed by a change of environment'.

Faith in Human Nature

Gandhiji declared himself to be 'an irrepressible optimists'. His optimism rested upon his belief in the infinite possibilities of the individual to develop non-violence. 'The more you develop it in your own being, the more infections it becomes, till it overwhelms your surroundings and . . . over sweep the world'. The very basis of the philosophy of non-violence is grounded on the belief in the efficacy of conversion as a method of winning the opponent. It was one of his fundamental believes. In 1920, he said, 'I refuse to suspect human nature'. In 1926 he said, 'The most practical, the most dignified way of going on in the world is to take people at their word, when you you no positive reason to the contrary, I refuse to believe that the tendency of the human nature is always downward'. A few months later he declared, 'Men like me cling to their faith in human nature . . . all appearances to the contrary not withstanding'.

Gandhiji placed man above institutions. He observed, 'Man and his deed are two distinct things. It is quite proper to resist and attack a system, but to resist and attack its author is tantamount to resisting and attacking oneself. For we are all tarred with the same brush, and are children of the one and the same creator and as such the divine powers within us are infinite. To slight a human being is to slight those divine powers, and thus to harm not only that being but with him the whole world'. In *Young India*, he said, 'I have discovered, that man is superior to the system he propounded. And so I feel, that Englishman, as individuals, are infinitely better than the system they have evolved as a corporation'.

Human Perfectability

Gandhiji did not expect complete realisation of the ideal. Though 'Human life is a series of compromises and it is not always easy to achieve in practice what one had found to be true in theory'. He exhorted not to lower the ideal of human development. 'Let us be sure of our ideal. We shall ever fail to realise it, but never cease to realise it'. He believed that 'satisfaction' lies in the effort, not in the attainment. 'Full effort is full victory'. 'The virtue of an ideal consists in its boundlessness. But although religious ideals must thus from their very nature remain unattainable by imperfect human being, although by virtue of their boundlessness they may seem ever to recede farther and farther away from us, the nearer we go to them, still they are closer to us than our very hands and feet because we are more certain of their reality and truth than even our own physical being. This faith in ideal constitutes real life, in fact, it is man's all in all'.

Man according to Gandhiji will ever remain imperfect, and it will always be his part to be perfect. He knew that man at the present state of his being was not perfect, but that did not negate the theoretical possibility of further development which amounted to his perfectibility. This idea of human perfectibility is a key-point for the philosophy of non-violence. And this belief logically leads to the conclusion of conversion and remaking of man. He said, 'In the application of the method of non-violence, one must believe in the possibility of every person, however depraved, being reformed under humane and skilled treatment'. In *Harijan* he said, 'When I was a little child, there used to be two blind performers in Rajkot. One of them was a musician. When he played on his instrument his fingers swept the strings with an unerring instinct and everybody listened spell-bound to his playing. Similarly, there are chords in every human heart. If we only know how to strike the right chord, we bring out the music'. The rationality of human nature is the pre-condition for its theoretical perfectibility.

A believer in rebirth, it was only natural for Gandhiji to believe that moral progress made in this life would be of avail to us in the after-life. Thus his faith in human perfectibility was not merely a moral conviction, but was ultimately based upon his metaphysical assumptions.

The Nature of Man

'Man is a complex multi-dimensional being including within him different elements of matter, life, consciousness, intelligence, and the divine spark'. At different times because of different influences, the whole of human nature has been seen by the wise and exalted from the point of view of this phase or that phase of man giving rise to different concepts of man.

Astronomical concept of man looks at man as a tiny physical process lost in the vast encompassing spaces of a galactic universe. Biological concept of Man focuses him as a being and regards him as the last stage of a protracted planetary evolution. Animalistic concept of Man concentrates upon his elementary appetites. Divine concept of Man interprets the individuals whole being in terms of a relation to Eternal Spirit.

Gandhian Concept of Man

Communism stresses the economic aspect of human nature and

democracy idealises the libertarian concept of man, Gandhiji idealises the spiritual aspect of man. Gandhiji believed that man is not merely a bundle of flesh and bones, but something more than and beyond this. Behind all this visible but unconscious matter, there is a spirit, a soul, indivisible, eternal, all-pervading and self-conscious. It is a part and parcel of God. In other words, it is Godhead within him.

The Dignity of Personality

For Gandhiji, 'the individual is the one supreme consideration'. Personality is sacred because the soul in man is part of God. In fact, what is reality in man is only the soul; he is nothing but Brahman. Gandhiji's belief in the *advaita* doctrine that there is but one Brahman in all, whether it be human or sub-human beings, means that all living beings are bound together inseparately to God. It makes man the servant of God's creation and not its lord. Gandhiji believes that 'if one man gains spiritually, the whole world gains with him and if one man falls, the whole world falls to that extent'. This is a conclusion of great significance since we find in it a powerful plea for universal education and for the oftenly observed fact that sometimes one great person exalts so many and sometimes person corrupt one corrupts so many.

Equality of Man

Gandhiji believes in equality between man and man. His concept of equality of man is also derived from the concept of the universal soul. He says, 'In my opinion there is one such thing as inherited or acquired superiority. I believe in rock bottom doctrine of *advaita* and my interpretation of advaita excludes my idea of superiority, at any state whatsoever. . . . I believe implicitly that all men are born equal. All whether in India or in England or America or in any circumstances whatever have the same soul as any other. . . I consider that it is unmanly for any person to claim superiority over a fellow being. . . . He who claims superiority at once forfeits his claim to be called a man'. This is in the line with christian belief that man's worth arises not from his civic status but from his being a child of God. 'Because children of God, all men are brothers'. Gandhiji's letter to the Rev. Keithan makes this concept of equality clearer still. He says, 'All men are born equal, out of it one is much stronger or weaker than another physically and mentally. Therefore, superficially there is no equality between the two. But there is an essential equality. In our nakedness God is not going to think of me as Gandhi or you as Keithan. And what are we in this mighty universe? We are less than atoms, and as between atoms there is no use asking which is bigger. Inherently, we are equal. The difference of race and skin; of mind and body, and of climate and nature are transitory'. Gandhiji's disarming humility and his gross identification with the masses, the poor and the downtrodden stem from this kind of thinking.

Free Will Vs Pre-Determination

Gandhiji's notion of the presence of God in man amounts to another belief that man has free will, reason, conscience and love. Man is the maker of his destiny. If he chooses to use his reason correctly and guides his life by listening to the dictates of his conscience and lives with his fellow beings with love in his heart, he can realise God and bring heaven on earth.

Gandhiji believes that, though our will is free, we cannot command results, we can only strive. Man can change temperament, can control it, but certainly, not eradicate it. God has not given so much liberty. If the leopard can change its spots, then only can man modify the peculiarities of his spiritual constitution. Of course, he can counter-act the effects of past mistakes by attaining complete detachment but inspite of the greatest effort of his environment or his upbringing. While conceding that people are controlled by their environment, Gandhiji would like them to live by self-direction and not by mere habit. In other words, he would like them to live as 'persons' acting at the moral level. He does not believe in complete freedom which might enable man to sever himself from or transcend nature. Such freedom can mean only chaos. He does not favour freedom that detracts from the moral path.

The Self in Self-expression

Gandhiji points out that purity of means is the only safe means to minimise evil . . . in order to overcome evil, one must stand wholly outside it, i.e., on the firm solid ground of unadulterated good.

Man's body is a product of nature and so, physical. But, Consciousness, reason, will, emotion and such other qualities and powers which man has are the expression of the spirit of soul. The true self is this spirit; not the finite self, with its lust and passions. When Gandhiji preaches self-expression, the 'self' is used in this restricted sense and not in the sense in which the term is used by the Naturalists. The false self should not be allowed to express itself. 'If man yields to the temptation, say Prof. Jeffreys, to subside on the natural level, he makes a beast of himself; and the beastliness of man is something quite different from the naturalness of the beast'. But if he wills, man can follow the spiritual path, and become more and more like God in love, goodness and abiding joy; for the divine powers within us are infinite.

Progress of Man

As a believer in the theory of evolution, Gandhiji is conscious of man's animal origin and so, he does not subscribe to the Wordsworthian view that the child comes from heaven. He says, 'We were perhaps all originally brutes. I am prepared to believe that we have become men by slow process of evolution from the brute'. Further, 'Man must choose either of the two courses, the upward or the downward; but as he has brute in him, he will more easily choose the downward course than the upward, especially, if the downward course is presented to him in a beautiful garb . . . the downward instinct is embodied in them'. Thus Gandhiji concludes that every one of us is a mixture of good and evil, the difference between the culture and brute being only a question of degree. So long as man is in the flesh even the greatest man can only be imperfect. 'There is no one without faults, not even men of God. They are men of God not because they are faultless but because they know their own faults . . . and are ever ready to correct themselves'. The glory is that man is not mere brute. He is above all, the soul and so, even the more brute of men has potentiality for goodness. It is this self-conscious impulse to realise the God inherent in him that distinguished man from the beast.

The Summum Bonum of Life

According to Gandhiji, 'there is no contradiction between God and man, as well as in the lower order of creation. Soul transcends time and space and unifies all apparently separate existence'. He also believes that 'human beings are working consciously or unconsciously towards the realisation of spiritual identity'. He says that 'life is an inspiration. Its mission is to strive after perfection, which is self-realisation. What I want to achieve — what have been striving and pining these thirty years, is self-realisation — to see God face to face, to attain *Moksha*. I live and move and have my belief in pursuit of this goal'.

This is the ideal which he prescribes for all. Because 'the soul is one in all, its possibilities are, therefore, the same for every one'. Gandhiji says, 'I wear the same corruptible flesh that the weakest of my fellows wear, and am, therefore, as liable to err as any'. Therefore, the ideals that regulate my life are presented for acceptance by mankind in general. I have arrived at them by gradual evolution. . . . I have not the shadow of a doubt that any man or woman cannot achieve what I have if he or she would make the same effort and cultivate the same hope and faith. . . . And I claim that what I practise, is capable of being practised by all because I am very ordinary mortal open to the same temptations and liable to the same weaknesses as the least among us'.

Thus Gandhiji believes that self-realisation is possible in and through society because he believes in 'the absolute oneness of humanity' and therefore to him, there is complete identity between him and humanity. So the goal of life-self-realisation cannot be attained unless *Sarvodaya* is materialised.

To conclude, Gandhiji emphasises the spiritual nature of man and he believes in the exercise of free will as well as the effect of environment. According to him, the *summum bonum* of man's life is self-realisation.

4

GANDHIAN APPROACH TO POPULATION

ONE OF the greatest crisis that man in this planet is facing today is the rate of growth of world's population. There has been a great deal of discussion in recent years about the population explosion. It is feared that a widespread famine is inevitable in the near future because of the rapid increase of the human population. People have been debating a great deal about the methods to be adopted to slow down the growth of population. Many people have strong feelings about the right to have children and it is considered than an interference with the natural birth rate is immoral. Others see the population control movement as an attempt of wealthy people to keep what they have and hold down the rest of the world in the process. On the other side some maintain that continued high birth rates are immoral, for they will lead to misery and starvation for millions.

The consequences of population growth on the development of underdeveloped countries are not the same because the conditions prevailing in these countries are quite different from those of developed economics. These economics are poor capital-scare and labour-abundant. Population growth has been supposed to be an obstacle to economic development in them. Rapid population growth increase the pressure of population on land and leads to mass unemployment in underdeveloped countries. The problem of feeding teeming millions becomes serious. There is greater pressure on educational and health facilities which are not adequately met. Population pressure also tends to accentuate the balance of payments problem. Food, consumer goods, raw materials, capital equipment, etc., are required to be imported to meet the ever increasing demand of the growing population. The rapid population growth depresses per capita incomes, lowers the standard of living and brings down the rate of capital formation. The consequences of rapid population growth on the development of underdeveloped countries are discussed below.

Population and Per Capita Income

The effect of population growth on per capita income is unfavourable. The growth of population tends to retard the per capita income in three ways: (1) It increases the pressure of population on land. (2) It leads to a rise in costs of consumption goods because of the scarcity of the cooperant factors to increase their supplies. (3) It leads to a decline in the accumulation of a capital because with increase in family members, expenses increases. These adverse effects of population growth on per capita income operate more severely if the percentage of children in the total population is high, as is actually the case in all the underdeveloped countries of the world. Every increase in national output is accompanied by a large number of consumers. A large number of children in the population entails a heavy burden on the economy, for, these children simply consume and do not add to national product. Another factor is the low expectancy of life in underdeveloped countries. Thus the effect of population growth is to lower the per capita income.

Population and Standard of Living

A rapidly increasing population leads to an increased demand for food products, clothes, etc. But their supplies cannot be increased in the short run due to the lack of cooperant factors, such as raw materials, skilled labour, capital, etc. Consequently their costs and prices rise which raise the cost of living of the masses. This brings down further the already low standard of living. Poverty breeds large number of children which increases poverty further and the vicious circle of poverty, more children and low standard of living continues. Thus the consequence of population growth is to lower the standard of living.

Population and Agricultural Development

In underdeveloped countries, people mostly live in rural areas. Agriculture is their main occupation. So with population growth the land-man-ratio is disturbed. Pressure of population on land increases because the supply of land is inelastic. It adds to disguised unemployment and reduces per capita productivity further. Low per capita productivity reduces the propensity to save and invest. As a result, the use of improved techniques and other improvements on land are not possible. Capital formation in agriculture suffers and the economy is bogged down to the subsistence level. The problem of feeding the additional population becomes serious due to acute shortage of food products. These have to be imported which accentuate the balance of payments difficulties. Thus the growth of population retards agricultural development and creates a number of other problems.

Population and Employment

A rapidly increasing population plunges the economy into mass unemployment and underemployment. As population increases the proportion of workers to total population rises. But in the absence of complementary resources, it is not possible to expand jobs. The result is that with the increase in labour force, unemployment and underemployment increase. A rapidly increasing population reduces incomes, savings and investment. Thus capital formation is retarded and job opportunities are reduced thereby increasing unemployment. Moreover, as the labour force increases in relation to land, capital and other resources, complementary factors available per worker decline, and as a result unemployment and underemployment increase. Underdeveloped countries have a backlog of unemployment which keeps on growing with a rapidly increasing population. This tends to raise the level of unemployment manifold as compared with the actual increase in labour force. For instance, the backlog of unemployed has increased with every five-year plan in India. The remedy is not only to increase employment opportunities for the current as well as the backlog of the employed people but to control population.

Population and Social Infrastructure

Rapidly growing population necessitates large investments in social infrastructure and diverts resources from directly productive assets. Due to scarcity of resources, it is not possible to provide educational, health, medical, transport and housing facilities to the entire population. There is overcrowding everywhere. As a result, the quality of these services goes down. 'Large numbers mitigate against an improvement in the quality of the population as productive agents. The rapid increase in school-age population and the expanding number of labour force entrants put ever-greater pressure on educational and training facilities and retard improvement in the quality of education. Similarly, too dense a population or a rapid rate of increase of population aggravates the problem of improving the health of population.' All this entails colossal investment.

Population and Labour Force

The labour force in an economy is the ratio of working population to total population. Assuming 50 years as the average life expectancy in an underdeveloped country, the labour force is in effect the number of people in the age-group of 15-50 years. During the demographic transitional phase the birth rate is high and the death rate is on the decline. The result is that a larger percentage of the total population is in the lower age-group of 1-15 years, and hence a smaller percentage comprises the labour force. A large percentage of children in the labour force is a heavy burden on the economy. On the other hand, a small labour force implies that comparatively there are few persons to participate in productive employment. Even if the birth rate starts declining, the labour force available for productive employment during the short run would be the same. However, the number of children would decline and this would have the effect of increasing the national income because the number of consumers would also fall. But this is only possible after the demographic transition stage is overcome which is not possible till the underdeveloped countries bring down their fertility rates. It does not mean that with their present high birth rates and low death rates, the labour force is not increasing in underdeveloped countries. It simply means that the addition to the lower age-group is larger than in the working age-group. Thus the labour force tends to increase with the increase in population.

Population and Capital Formation

Population growth retards capital formation. As population increases, per capita available income declines. People are required to feed more children with the same income. It means more expenditure on consumption and a further fall in the already low savings, and consequently in the level of investment.

The increase in population will also lead to the diversion of capital investments from directly productive activities to social overhead capital. The rapidly increasing population will have to be provided more basic facilities in the form of schools, roads, hospitals, water, etc., which do not add to the national product directly and immediately, with the result that the growth rate of the economy remains at the lower level. The return on capital invested is high in directly productive activities as against social overhead capital. So capital formation is adversely affected with the diversion of governmental resources from their more productive uses to current uses to provide the people for their more urgent needs. Public savings and capital formation will decline in another way as a result of a rapidly growing population. When income decline and consumption expenditures increase, it is difficult for the government to levy taxes on the people. Certain exemptions from taxes have to be given to the people. As a result, state revenues decline which reduce investment and capital formation unless some other alternative measures are adopted by the government. A rapidly growing population by lowering the rate of capital formation keeps the level of technology at a low level. Or we may say, a rapidly rising population by lowering incomes, savings and investment compels the people to use a low level technology which retards capital formation.

The consequences of a rapidly increasing population are to retard all development effort in an underdeveloped country unless accompanied by high rates of capital accumulation, and technological progress. But these factors are not available and the result is that population explosion leads to declining agricultural productivity, low per capita income, low living standards, mass unemployment, and low rate of capital formation.

Population and Women

M. Amara Jyothi in his research on population control has come out with the suggestion that for this great task the attitude of women will have great influence. His analysis of the educated and uneducated women, indicates that irrespective of their religions, almost all the uneducated women have got negative attitude towards small family. Some women even refused to think about it. In some cases, even though the men were willing to be operated, their wives even refused it. In some other cases, they felt that they have to obey the wishes of husbands and relatives.

Among the educated women all of them have got positive attitudes, but the degree varies depending upon the religion. Hindu women are most positive than Muslims and Christians. The reason for this lesser positive attitudes among women of Muslim and Christian religions may be that they belong to minority community and they feel that their security in society increases in proportion to the rise in their number. The other reason among the uneducated for preferring a large family may be because that they feel that a large family is a security for old age and prosperity for the present.

The need of the hour is to create an awareness among women about the various benefits of the small family and how in turn it affects the development and prosperity of a country and quality of life. They should also be made conscious of population growth and starvation in India and the need of controlling population. The other way is to provide security to couples through a national social security scheme to support them in their old age or on loss of an earning member. This scheme will relieve most of the weaker sections, of the feeling, that they don't have any sort of security in hard times.

Gandhian Approach to Population

The population explosion in India is a twentieth century phenomenon. Previously when industry had not so improved and also the medical care, there was no problem of over-population, no scarcity of land and population growth was no hindrance to the development of society. But India has encountered an enormous increase of population in the present century an increase which is continuing now at the rate of 13 million per year. This has exercised tremendous pressure on the limited resources of the country. No doubt the country has advanced much in economic field especially during the past thirty-five years. Yet, in spite of it, her problems are staggering and her poverty more pervasive than before, mainly because of the unprecedented increase in population number.

In 1920, Gandhiji wrote in *Young India* about the growing population of the country: 'I must not conceal from the reader the sorrow I feel when I hear of births in mind. I must confess that for years I have contemplated with satisfaction the prospect suspending procreation by voluntary self-denial. India is ill-equipped today for taking care even for her present population'. When Gandhiji made this observation, the population of India was 250 million. Today it has passed beyond the 800 million mark; it has resulted in increasing unemployment, poverty and misery.

The following are Gandhiji's observations about over-population and its control: 'if it is contended that birth-control is necessary for the nation because of over-population, I dispute the proposition. It has never been proved. In my opinion, by a proper land system, better agriculture and a supplementary industry, this country is capable of supporting twice as many people as there are in it today'. 'The bogey of increasing birth-rate is not a new thing. It has been often trotted out. Increase in population is regulated or restricted by artificial methods is a calamity of the first grade whether we know it or not. It is bound to degrade the race if it becomes universal, which, thank God, it is never-likely to be. Pestilence, wars and famines are cursed antidotes against cursed trust which is responsible for unwanted children. If we would avoid this three-fold curse, we would avoid too the curse of unwanted children by the sovereign remedy of self-control. The evil consequences of artificial methods are being seen by discerning men even now. Without, however encroaching upon the moral domain, let me say that propagation of the race rabit-wise must undoubtedly be stopped; but not so as to bring greater evils in its train. It should be stopped by methods which in themselves ennoble the race. In other words, it is all a matter of proper education which would embrace every department of life; and dealing with one curse will take in its orbit all the others. A way is not to be avoided because it is upward and therefore uphill. Man's upward progress means ever-increasing difficulty which is to be welcomed.'

Population Ethics – A Hindu Perspective

As an agricultural and rural population, the Hindu Community has been generally in favour of a large family. This was mainly due to the fear of infant mortality and the desire for the male issue. But now that the modern medicine and health has taken care of infant mortality, it has declined sharply and is steadily decreasing further. The death rate has also continued to diminish and shows still a downward trend.

Population growth is posing a practical and moral challenge to the followers of every religious tradition in India, and especially to Hindus, who constitute 80 per cent of all Indians. The Hindus are naturally obliged to reconsider some of their traditional attitudes towards family, caste and society, and make some innovations, within their tradition, favourable to population control and the small family norm.

Principles of Hindu Ethics

Hindu ethics covers the well-being of man not only in this world but also his life in the 'Other World' after death. It contains a code of life and a philosophy of social and ethical relations; it aims at righteous, economic well-being, aesthetic enjoyment and spiritual salvation.

The ambition of the Hindu father came to be to produce a son, physically as strong as a stone or an axe and intellectually as brilliant as gold, with a lifespan covering a hundred autumns. The ambition of a Hindu girl was to be wife of a hero and the mother of a hero. Manu says, "By the birth of the first alone, man pays off his ancestral debt . . . only he is born of *dharma*, righteousness; the rest are born of *Kama*, 'Passion'." Actually a son and a daughter would fulfil the religious, social and emotional needs of a Hindu couple.

The basis of population control should not be merely a higher standard of life or longer life, but it should be better life. The quality of life consists in the contributions it can make to the traditional values and ideals of householders, the loving care of family and children, respect for women, service of once community, the welfare of posterity, and the moral and spiritual progress of human personality. Hindu insights such as discipline, sacrifice, compassion, and contentment can advantageously used to motivate people to the acceptance of the small family norm.

Abstinence

Hindu customs have laid down principles regarding the rules of sexual abstinence for householder. Widow remarriage is prohibited in Hindu society and also intercourse among the married during certain periods and religious days. Though Hindu community has started having the awareness about the need of birth control, Gandhiji's insistence does not seem find acceptance among them.

The other solution is in the postponement of marriage for both. If the marriage age of females in India especially among the Hindus rises to twenty years, the birth rate is likely to decline by thirty per cent. With the introduction of free education and higher education the age of marriage among urban and, educated girls have risen in recent years. But there are still a vast number of rural females who do not go to schools. Spread of literacy and education among both males and females is a sure, though slow remedy for over-population. Perhaps the ancient custom of *swayamvara* can be advantageously used in this regard.

Contraception

Brahadaranyaka Upanishad spells out a method of birth control for man 'who desires his wife, but does not want her to conceive'. Shastras recommend a temperature exercise of the sex instinct by the householder and contraception since avoids unwanted and undesirable pregnancies can be and is generally accepted by the Hindus.

Abortion

Abortion is legal in India for the purpose of saving the life of a woman. But Hindus in general look upon it as sinful and it amounts to taking the life of a sentiment being. Compassion for suffering women demands a reconsideration of the traditional attitude toward unwanted pregnancies. The general attitude however, is likely to continue to be in favour of conception rather than the abortion of an unwanted conception.

Sterilisation

Sterilisation is a reliable and uncomplicated method of family planning. Gandhiji did not approve of it except in cases of individuals with chronic diseases. It has neither religious nor moral sanction and compulsory sterilisation violates human personality and creates psychological and social problems. But it can be made available to both males and females under two conditions: (a) it should be voluntary and (b) since it is irreversible, it should be available only to those parents who have one or two children to satisfy their religious and social requirements.

Thus we find that Hindu ethics is large and elastic and the Hindus should find no difficulty in adopting one of the many methods of family planning. Especially contraception is permissible in Hindu society; it is to be encouraged in Hindu ethics.

Gandhiji's Views on Artificial Control of Birth

Gandhiji felt that the modern artificial methods of controlling the size of the family are not proper and they are leading to disastrous results. He says, 'Procreation is a natural phenomenon indeed, but within specific limits. A transgression of these limits imperils womankind, emasculates the race, induces diseases, puts a premium on voice and makes world ungodly'. Further, 'If contraceptives are restored to, frightful results will follow. Men and women will be living for sex alone. They will become soft-brained, unhinged in fact, mental and moral recks'.

Gandhiji's Four-point Programme

Gandhiji, by all these arguments, did not mean that he was against all types of quantitative controls of population. The difference between him and the westerners is that he wanted to control the growth of population irrespective of the size, the natural resources and the stage of development of the country and through less injurious methods. This is evident from his views on marriage and *Brahmacharya.*

Late Marriage

Gandhiji, from his own experience had come to know the pitfalls of early marriage. He was married at the age of thirteen. Many years later when he was looking at the experiences of sex life in his early years, it was with a same remorse that he did. He thought that perhaps the undesirable traits he saw in his eldest son were an echo of his own undisciplined and unformulated early life. He called himself and his wife as 'married children' to denote how raw and immature their life had been in that married state. So he considered that such marriages to be null and void and as such no marriage at all. Such early marriages affect the rate of growth of population adversely but also affects the health of the partners because of over-indulgence. Besides, being children themselves they will not be able to bring up the children in a proper way. Because of these circumstances, he left also that a child widow was not in reality a widow, but a maiden and must be treated as such.

In his advice to students in *Young India*, Gandhiji writes: 'You must be able surely to control your best to this extent, that you are not going to marry a girl that is under 16 years of age. If I could . . . . Twenty years is early enough even in India. It is we who are responsible for the precocity of girls, not even the Indian climate, because we know girls of the age of 20 who are pure and undefiled and able to stand the storm that may rage round. Let us not hung that precocity to ourselves. Some Brahmin students tell me that they cannot follow this principle, that they cannot get Brahmin girls sixteen years old, very few Brahmins keep their daughters unmarried till that age, the Brahmin girls are married mostly before 10, 12 and 13 years. Then he say to Brahmin youth, cease to be a Brahmin, if you cannot possibly control yourself. Choose a grown up girl of 16 who became a widow, when she was a child. If you cannot get a Brahmin widow who has reached that age then go and take any girl you like. And I tell you that the god of the Hindus will pardon that boy 'who preferred to marry out of his caste rather than ravish a girl of twelve. When your heart is not pure and you cannot master your passions, you cease to be an educated man'.

Brahmacharya

The second formula which Gandhiji gave was *Brahmacharya.* Explaining its meaning and importance he says: 'Let us remember the root meaning of *Brahmacharya. Brahmacharya* means course of conduct adopted to the reach of Truth. From this eytomological meaning arises a special meaning i.e., control of all the senses. We must forget the incomplete definition which restricts itself to the sexual aspect only'. '*Brahmacharya* is not merely mechanical celibacy, it means complete control over all the senses and freedom from lust in thought, word and deed. As such it is a royal road to self-realisation or attainment of Brahma'. *Brahmacharya* teaches self-control not only of desire for sex but also of other senses. This all round self-control raises the moral fibre of the nation and removes variety, anger, fear and jealousy from the people'.

'*Brahmacharya* is a mental state. It is undoubtedly helped by abstiniousmen in all respects. But diet plays the least part in giving one the necessary mental state. Not the wrong diet will not hinder progress. What I want to say is that the right diet taken in moderation is not the only thing in the observance of *Brahmacharya* though it is undoubtedly one of the necessary things. Indulgence of the palate will be the surest sign of a weak mental state which is repugnant to *brahmacharya.* The sovereign remedy for the *brahmacharya* is realisation that the soul is a part of the Divine and that the Divine resides within us. A heart grasp of this fact induces mental purity and strength. You should therefore read such books as would enable you to grasp the central fact, cultivate such companionship as would constantly make you think of the Divine presence and follow all the directions given about fresh air, hip-baths, etc., in my book entitled 'Self-restraint *vs* Self-indulgence'. And when you are doing all these things regularly and industriously, do not brood over all that happens, but have confidence that success is bound to attain your effort'.

Need for Brahmacharya: Regarding the need for *Brahmacharya*, Gandhiji observed, 'A large part of the miseries of today can be avoided if we look at the relations between the sexes in a healthy and pure light, and regard overselves as trustees for the moral welfare of the future generations'. 'Life without *brahmacharya* appears to me to be insipid and animal-like. The brute by nature knows no self-restraint. What formerly appeared to me to be extravagant praise of *brahmacharya* in our religious books seems now, with increasing clearness everyday, to be absolutely proper and founded of experience'. 'I hold that a life of perfect continence in thought, speech and action is necessary for reaching spiritual perfection. And a nation that does not possess such men is poorer for the want'.

'He whose heart is pure has the all-purifying waters of the Ganga in his house. For one whose thought is under control the other is mere child's play. The *Brahmachari* of my conception will be healthy and will easily live long. He will not even suffer from so much as a headache. Mental and physical work will not cause fatigue. He is ever bright, never slothful. Outward neatness will be an exact reflection of the inner. He will exhibit all the attributes of the steadfast one described in the *Gita*. It needs cause no worry if not one person is met with answering the description'. 'So long as thought is not under complete control of the will, *brahmacharya* in its fullness is absent. Involuntary thought is an affection of the mind; and curbing of thought, therefore, means curbing of the mind which is more difficult to curb than the wind. Nevertheless the existence of God within makes even control of the mind possible. Let no one think that it is impossible because it is difficult. It is the highest goal, and it is no wonder that the highest effort should be necessary to attain it'.

Gandhiji says that mind is the most important instrument in the practice of *Brahmacharya*. He says, '*Brahmacharya*, like all other observances, must be observed in thought, word and deed. We are told in the *Gita*, and experience will corroborate the statement, that the foolish man, who appears to control his body, but is nursing evil thoughts is his mind, makes a vain effort. It may be harmful to suppress the body, if the mind is at the same time allowed to go astray. Where the mind wanders, the body must follow sooner or later. It is one thing to allow the minds to harbour impure thoughts; it is a difficult thing altogether, if it strays among them in spite of ourselves. Victory will be ours in the end, if we non-cooperate with mind in its evil wanderings'.

Inner condition is essential to control the mind. To quote Gandhiji, '*Brahmacharya* is a mental condition. The outward behaviour of a man is at once the sign and proof of the inner state. He who has killed the sexual urge in him will never be guilty of it in any shape or form. However attractive a woman may be her attraction will produce no effect on man without the urge. The same rule applies to woman'. '*Brahmacharya* is not a virtue that can be cultivated by outward restraints. He who runs away from a necessary contact with a woman does not understand the full meaning of *brahmacharya*. The true *brahmachari* will shun fake restraints. He must create his own fences according to his limitations, breaking them down when he feels that they are unnecessary. The first thing is to know what true brahmacharya is, then to realise its value and lastly to cultivate this priceless virtue. I hold that true service of the country demands this observance'.

Control of Sense

'Mere control of animal passion has been thought to be tantamount to observing *brahmacharya*. I feel that this conception is complete and wrong. *Brahmacharya* means control of all organs of sense. He who attempts to control only one organ and allows all others free play is bound to find his effort futile. . . . To hear suggestive stories with the ears, to see suggestive sights with the eyes, to taste stimulating food with the tongue, to touch exciting things with the hands, and then at the same time, expect to control the only remaining organ is like putting one's hand in the fire, and expecting to escape being burnt. He therefore, who is resolved to control the one must be otherwise determined to control the rest. . . . I have always felt that much harm has been done by the narrow definition of brahmacharya. If we practise simultaneous control in all directions, the attempt will be scientific and possible of success. Perhaps the palate is the chief sinner'.

Gandhiji cites his own example for striving for *brahmacharya*. In his autobiography, 'For me observance of even bodily *brahmacharya* has been full of difficulties. Today I am to say that I feel myself fairly safe, but I have yet to achieve complete mastery over thought, which is so essential. Not that the will or effort is lacking, but it is yet a problem to me wherefrom undesirable thoughts spring their insidious invasion. . . . I have no doubt that there is a key to lock out undesirable thoughts, but everyone has to find it out for himself. Saints and seers have left their experiences for us, but they have given us no infallible and universal prescription. For perfection or freedom from error comes only from grace, and so seekers after god have left us *mantras* such as *Ramanama*, hallowed by their own austerities and charged with their purity . . . without an unreserved surrender to his grace, complete mastery over thought is impossible. This is the teaching of every great book of religion, and I am realising the truth of it every moment of my striving after that perfect *Brahmacharya*'.

In *Harijan* Gandhiji says, 'I have practised *brahmacharya* for over thirty years with considerable success though luring in the midst of activities. After the decision to lead the life of a *brahmachari*, there was little change in my outward practice, except with my wife. My *brahmacharya* was not derived from books. I evolved my own rules for my guidance and that of those who, at my invitation, had formed me in the experiment. If I have followed the prescribed restrictions, much less have I accepted the description found even in religious literature of woman as the source of all evil and temptations. Owing as I do all the good there may be in me to my mother. I have looked upon woman, never as an object of satisfaction of sexual desire, but always with the veneration due to my own mother. Man is the temptor and aggressor. It is not woman whose touch defiles man but he is often himself too impure to touch her. I am experimenting. I have never claimed to have been a perfect brahmachari of my definition. I have not acquired that control over my thoughts that I need for my researches on non-violence. If my non-violence is to be contageous and infectious, I must acquire greater control over my thoughts'.

'From that day when I began *brahmacharya*, our freedom began. My wife became a free woman, free from my authority and her lord and master, and I became free from the slavery to my own appetite which she had to satisfy. No other woman had any attraction for me in the same sense that my wife had. I was too loyal to her as husband and loyal to the vow I had taken before my mother to be no slave to any other woman. But the manner in which my *brahmacharya* came to me irresistibly drew me to woman as the mother of man. She became too sacred for sexual love. And so every woman at once became sister or daughter to me'. 'If I were sexually attracted towards women, I have courage enough, even at this time of life, to become a polygamist. I do not believe in free love. I have looked upon it as dog's love. Secret love, is, besides, cowardly'.

In *Navajivan* on 5th May, 1924, Gandhiji replied to some inquiries regarding *brahmacharya*. He said, '. . . I am sorry to say that I have not yet reached that perfect state of *brahmacharya*, though I am every moment of my life striving to reach it. I have not given up hope of reaching that state in this very body. I have gained control over body. I can be master of myself during my waking hours. I have fairly succeeded in learning to control my tongue. But I have yet to cover many stages in the control of my thoughts. They do not come and go at my bidding. My mind is thus constantly in a state of insurrection against itself.

In my waking moments, however, I can stop my thoughts from colliding with one another. I may say that in the waking state the mind is secure against the approach of evil thoughts. But in the hours of sleep, control over the thoughts is much less. When asleep, the mind would be swayed by all sorts of thoughts, by unexpected dreams, and by desire for things done and enjoyed by the flesh before. Such thoughts or dreams when unclean are followed by the worse consequences. Whilst such experiences are possible person cannot be said to be free from all passions. The deviation, is however diminishing, but has not yet ceased. If I had complete mastery over my thoughts, I should not have suffered from the diseases of pleurisy, dysentry and appendicitis that I did during the last ten years. I believe that a healthy soul should inhabit a healthy body. . . .

I have said so much about myself for the simple reason that my correspondents and others like them may have patience and self-confidence. The soul is one in all. Its possibilities are therefore the same for every one. With some, it has manifested itself, with others it has yet to do so. Patience striving would carry every one through and to the same experience.'

Self-Control

As against the evils of artificial methods of birth-control which he considered as sin, Gandhiji advocated self-control and abstinence. To quote Gandhiji, 'If we begin to believe that indulgence in animal passion is necessary, harmless and sinless, we shall want to give reins to it and shall be powerless to resist it. Whereas if we educate ourselves to believe that such indulgence is harmful, sinful, unnecessary and can be controlled, we shall discover that self-restraint is perfectly possible'. 'My quarrel with the advocates of contraceptives lies in their taking it for granted that ordinary mortals cannot exercise self-control. Some of them even go so far as to say that even if they can, they ought not to do so. To them, no matter how eminent they may be in their own sphere. I say, in all humility but with utmost confidence, they are talking without experience of the possibility of self-control. They have no right to limit the capacity of the human soul'.

International Migration

S.S. Gupta says that Gandhiji believed in international migration for population problem. This idea came to him when he was in South Africa and was thinking of the problems of the Indians there. He felt that due to rapid advancement of communication and transport, the world is shrinking fast and people are becoming more and more cosmopolitan in outlook. If migration of population is carried on the basis of mutual gains, the international relations will also improve and it will also bring the Mulatto dream nearer realisation. Hence not as labourers and inferiors and immigrants adopt the country they are migrating to us our own.

Conclusion

Gandhiji was a pragmatist. He was not sitting on a wrong tower. His feet were strongly rooted in the sand. He considered marriage as the spiritual union through physical. Marriage for sexual appetite was no marriage, for him. He said that undefiled love between husband and wife takes one nearer God than any other love. When sex is mixed with the undefiled love, it takes one away from ones Maker. The purpose of human birth is to realise God and defiled love or marriage of sex is an impediment in the path of the search of Brahman.

Gandhiji strove to see God face to face. Service to humanity was the path that led him to God. He felt that one who employs himself in service to humanity should never have time to think of family. This contemplation made him to take the celibacy vow. He knew and had confessed that the path of celibacy is like walking on the edge of a sword. Nevertheless he marched on towards the light undauntedly without casting a look backwards. He was of the opinion that once people's morality and their physical and moral well being was taken care of economic betterment will follow. Spirituality to him was the breath that sustained his life.

5

GANDHIAN CONCEPT OF HUMANISM

IN THE West Humanism is regarded as a philosophy which champions the cause of man's freedom and individuality against a theological world-view. Humanism was an intellectual movement which characterised Renaissance. It emphasised the dignity of man and his perfectability. Humanism began to develop in Italy in the 14th century and spread all over Europe in the 15th and 16th centuries. The famous English humanist was Sir Thomas More whose Utopia is famous.

The Concept of Human Nature

According to Gandhiji, the real individual is an immortal spiritual entity. Man is said to be divine spark. 'All persons are children of the same God', 'tarred with the same brush', and 'the divine powers within us are infinite'. Man is the citizen of the moral kingdom of ends and not mere mechanical and organic aggregation of physical forces and chemical elements. He has a sense of spiritual consciousness and moral internality. Being essentially spirit, he can rise superior to evil.

Gandhiji accepts that God as truth is the author only of goodness and never of sin, impurity, evil and falsehood. 'I cannot account for the existence of evil by any rational method. To want to do so is to be co-equal with God. I am therefore humble enough to recognise evil as such. And I call God long suffering and patient precisely because he permits evil in the world. I know that he has evil in him, and yet if there is evil, he is the author of it and yet untouched by it'.

Gandhiji never emphasised that evil should be conquered and eradicated. Hence such as Surdas and Tulsidas, Gandhiji always prayed to God for the divine mercy which alone could cleanse a man's heart. Although at the cosmic level, evil is inexplicable, at the individual level it could be traced to one's own actions. He traces the evil in man to his own evil *Samskaras* or past tendencies. 'I am a believer in previous births and re-births. All our relationships are the result of *Samskaras* we carry from our previous births. God's laws are inscrutable and are the subject of endless search. No one can fathom them'.

Gandhiji had deep faith in the goodness of man's nature in spite of the existence of evil because he accepted that it was possible to realise the triumph of divinity. He says, 'man is higher than the brute and has a divine mission to fulfil. . . . To find truth completely is to realise oneself and one's destiny'. Man's true aim is the conquest not of external nature but of his empirical self because the suppression of the lower self can alone vindicate the greatness of human spirit. Man is essentially good and for asserting this goodness he should advance in the path of self-conquest. But the belief in the fundamental and essential goodness and purity of the human soul does not imply that society is the sole breeding ground of contamination and perversity. There is no dominant conception in Gandhi of the vitiating and corrupting effects of society on the pure individual as in Rousseau. Both Gandhiji and Rousseau are agreed upon the inner goodness of human nature. But there is difference with regard to the source of depravities. According to Rousseau, contamination is brought about by reason and institutional convention. Gandhiji is more insistent on stressing that human depravity is due to one's past *Samskaras*. Thus he upholds a more individualistic view than Rousseau. But he also recognised the society's responsibility for several evils.

Since Gandhiji believed the inherent sinfulness of human nature as being psychological, he wanted to bring about a psychological regeneration of man to bring out the inherently divine nature in man. He said, 'Man in the flesh is essentially imperfect' and although he may be described as made in the image of God, he is far from being God, hence the task of moral education is to transmute the lower self of man into his higher ideal self. 'Human nature will only find itself when it fully realises that to be human it has to cease to be beastly or brutal.' Though we have the human folm, without the attainment of the virtue of non-violence, we still share the qualities of our remote reputed ancestor.

Gandhiji emphasised the necessity of constant efforts for the moral and spiritual remaking of man. He accepted the creative power of self-suffering human individuals and by his philosophical notion that incessant efforts for the perfection of individuality, he at the root of progress, he makes the exponents of modern thought aware of the significance of spiritual subjectivism. According to him, even social betterment depends upon individual efforts for self-purification.

This purification has to be attained by prolonged *sadhana* and grace of God. The potential *sattva* has to be actualised. This can be attained by cultivating *ahimsa* in the following three manners: (a) Resolute will to root out untruth and *Himsa,* (b) Constructive work and (c) basing domestic relations on *Ahimsa.*

Moral and spiritual goodness is acquired by a process of scrutiny, cultivation of character and the realisation of the sense of unity of living beings, only *seva* and *sadhana* can lead to the true moral evolution of man which is dependent upon the slow inwardisation of the great vows or *vratas* inculcated in the scriptures and accepted by Gandhiji for himself and the members of his *ashram.* Hence he emphasised the dignity and sanctity of the conscience of the individual and prescribed an internal judgement for the rightness or otherwise of human actions and motives. Thus moral evolution and not governmental coercion was the remedy.

Gandhiji also believed in touching the heart of his political opponent and had faith in the efficacy of the technique of appeal. He always appealed to man and especially to the *satvik* and divine in man. He always started with the *Atman* as a subjective entity.

Man is essentially a spirit. The spirit provides unity to the different phases of his existence and hence a comprehensive psycho-spiritual solution is needed. But this is dependent upon the energisation of moral sensibilities and feeling and hence the stress should always on the moral and spiritual aspect rather than on the intellectual, scientific and the institution. The fundamental and ultimate solution, of matter according to him, is the religious making of man, the human heart, he felt, holds the final key to all social and political dynamics.

Man has grown in the finer sensibilities from what he was in his primitive condition. The development of sentiments and emotions round the institution of the family is an additional testimony to the slow moral evolution of human nature. Even in the other realms of social, economic and political life there is evinced a slow tendency towards the lessening of the areas of conflict. Gandhiji stressed the technique of cultivation of altruistic virtues and feelings to bring about a change in human nature which implies the suppression of demonic elements.

Gandhiji's Spiritual Humanism

Gandhiji's Humanism was rooted in the realisation and spiritual experience of his whole being that all life was one and that life was but the manifestation and reflection of the reality itself.

For Gandhiji, the transcendental aspect of reality was a truth of inner experience no doubt. But its realisation in every day life was of immediate and paramount importance to him; that is why the truth of daily life, its experience through its own perception, observation, contemplation, and empathy were his pre-occupation. The individual has no other way of realising the truth of the totality of reality expect through social life and relationship with others. Therefore, whether it was the suffering of labourers in South Africa or peasants of Kaira or the insult of one nation exploiting another through imposition of slavery; they all evoked the utmost effort on the part of Gandhiji to serve the cause of suffering humanity.

Gandhiji identified with humanity, its joys and sorrows, its aspirations and inner seekings. He saw that it was through love alone he could serve it.

Gandhiji was a great devotee of God but he had also immense faith in man. There was no antithesis between his humanism and his belief in divine providence. He said, 'My faith is in God and therefore in the people'. Since there is no antithesis between God and man in him, he believed that the same soul, invisible, eternal, all pervading and self-conscious, run through lower as well as the higher orders of creation. 'I believe', he wrote, 'in absolute oneness of God and, therefore, also of humanity. . . . What though we have many bodies, we have but one soul'. It transcends time and space and unifies all apparently separate existence – God is organically bound up with mankind and all living beings. Hence love for man leads to the realisation of God.

Gandhiji was a humanist in two senses - first for what he did for the downtrodden to emancipate them and secondly for his faith in the redemption and regeneration of man.

The suffering of the Indian peasants brought forth all the agonies of his soul. Hence he tried to identify himself with the loneliest, the disinherited, the meek and the humblest. He cried, 'It is the greatest tragedy I know of there men and women, our brothers and sisters - dying a slow, torturing death. There is an eternal, occasionally with rice, they seem to mock us with the life they live'.

In his concern for the poor and the downtrodden and his exhortations for the betterment of their lot, Gandhiji named them as *Daridra Narayan*. He got this word from Deshbandhu C.R. Das. In the tattered bodies of the peasants and workers in Champaran, Gandhiji saw the concrete embodiment of God, truth and *ahimsa.* His overflowing love for the suffering and exploited humanity revealed his intense humanity. The essence of the humanist spirit is deep love of the people. Gandhiji's sincere love and regard for the people was an expression of humanism. He says, 'I will give a talisman. Whenever you are in doubt or when the self becomes too much with you, apply the following test. Recall the face of the poorest and the weakest man whom you may have seen and ask yourself, if the step you contemplate is going to be of any use to him. Will he gain anything by it? Will it restore him to control over his own life and destiny? In other words, will it lead to *Swaraj* for the hungry and spiritually starving millions?

It was this humanism that led him undertake the *satyagraha* in South Africa. It was again this humanism that led him undertake the other *satyagrahas* in his own motherland. Again it was only this humanism that made him live amidst the poor in his *ashrams* and made him a lovely pilgrim in a bloodshed alien land such as *Naokali.* His humanism inspired his sufferings in serving the sick and the leper. Like the Buddha of the ancient time, his humanism embraced God's all creations, not man alone. Like Jesus Christ, his humanism considered none his enemy, none his object of hatred. Even general Smuts who considered Gandhiji his political enemy testifies to his humanism as: 'However often he may differ from him, we are conscious all the time of his sincerity, his unselfishness and above all his fundamental and universal humanity. He always act as a great human, with deep sympathy for men of all classes and all races as especially the under-dog'.

Sarvodaya and Trusteeship

It is this humanism that gave rise to the principle of *Sarvodaya* and Trusteeship. He called upon the rich people to regard themselves as trustees of their wealth. *Sarvodaya* stands for the emancipation, the uplift and the elevation of all. It aims to serve the good of all and not merely the numerical majority. It is certainly, not opposed to the concept of social and economic equality. It is not merely a theory of ethical justice. It is emphatic in its quest also for distributive social and economic justice. In an era of the mad rush for power, the significance of *Sarvodaya* lies in stressing the permanent value of self-abhegation. It appeals to the mind and heart in terms of values and goals.

The philosophy and sociology of *Sarvodaya*, based on the insights and experience of Gandhiji is a reassertion of the valuational and moral approach to the problems of mankind, which has been a part of ancient Indian culture for ages. The philosophy and sociology of *Sarvodaya* can add the moral tonic to Indian civilisation. The greatest contribution of Sarvodaya lies in the reassertion of the Gandhian moral approach to the problems of man.

Gandhiji was a humanist because he had faith in redemption and regeneration of man. In 1946-47 due to the upsurge of communal frenzy on an unprecedented furious scale, he was little perturbed. He saw the edifice he had build with the ardent *Tapasya* of over twenty-five years tottering but was still hopeful. Like a profound spiritual humanist he wrote, 'you must not lose faith in humanity. . . . Humanity is an ocean; if a few drops of the ocean are dirty, the ocean does not become dirty'. The essence of spiritual humanism as enunciated by Gandhiji is to stress the significance of the universal values in man. The differences between men are apparent and superficial. The grave is the final destiny of all men. But fundamental spirit in man is undying and perennial. Hence all men should be treated with respect and decency and the dignity of all should be protected and defended. He pointed out, 'No human being is so bad as to be beyond redemption; no human being is so perfect as to warrant . . . considers to be wholly evil'. Gandhiji's adherence to the absolutism of truth and non-violence made him hostile to the destruction of life in any folm. Life postulates respect for it. He regarded all life as sacred. Human life is entitled to dignity, consideration and love.

Gandhi as a Humanist

Gandhiji's humanism was the pivot of all the different aspects of his wonderful personality. His humanism meant his utter devotion to the human interests-welfare of the individual men and women of the human race. According to Gandhiji, the highest service to man will be our sincere endeavour for drawing out the divine nature in man. To gain this end, we have to be in communion with God and to worship him as the source of all our noble virtues.

To serve man in his distress, in his poverty, in his illness and in his sorrows, to wipe out the tears for his eyes constitutes the true type of humanism and Gandhiji was the votary of this genuine type of humanism. To translate one's noblest thoughts into action is the highest achievement of man; Gandhiji's greatness rests on his achievement.

As morality has to be nurtured in the sort of religion so humanism also is rooted in the deep faith in God. Humanism bereft of its life-giving source of a living faith in God, withers like a flower-plant which has its roots taken off from the soil. Gandhiji's humanism was only a corollary of his realisation of the presence of God in all human beings in concrete shape and was ultimately based on the bed-rock of *Advaita* philosophy. He wrote, 'My creed is service to God and therefore of humanity'. In another context he said, 'I believed in *Advaita*, I believe in the essential unity of man and for that matter of all that lives'. His humanism is thus different from the pattern which is advocated by the modern atheists, who conceive it as something floating like a gossamer without any subsistence or a flowers-plant held aloft uprooted.

By virtue of his humanism Gandhiji attracted like a magnet, the people of different races, religions and creeds unto him and his followers in large numbers round him to form a happy family as it were. His humanity was undivided and he loved all men irrespective of caste, creed or colours.

Gandhiji's humanism was practical. He invariably put into practice first and then he preached it. He did not hesitate to risk his life even to serve the suffering humanity. Once when there was an outbreak of plague in Bombay, he came forward unhesitatingly to work as the chief organiser of the committee constituted for the purpose of teaching preventive measures to the people threatened by deadly diseases. During the times of the First World War Gandhiji offered his services for nursing the wounded soldiers although he did not support any welfare. His humanism admitted no hatred or enmity to anybody. He pardoned his assailant in South Africa and would not allow any legal action to be taken against him.

Gandhiji's heart went to the lowly and suffering. He gave up all luxuries voluntarily, to live the life of the poor. He would not even use a mosquito curtain as the poor of India had none. He used the cheapest and the simplest fare for his meal and travelled in third class, to realise the sorrow and suffering of the poor. He led a simple life to identify himself with the starving millions.

Gandhiji called untouchability a blot on Hinduism and tried his utmost to atone for the injuries which the caste Hindus meted out to them throughout the ages. He held that as humanity one and indivisible, he was responsible as a part and parcel of humanity for any sin committed by any other part. For this reason he resorted to fasts on so many occasions to atone for the sins of his fellow men.

In later days Gandhiji used to live in the Bhangi Colony at Delhi to feel like one of the untouchables. In 1924 he said, 'We must first come in living touch with them by working for them and in their midst. We must share their sorrows, understand their difficulties and anticipate their wants. With the pariahs we must be pariahs and see how we feel to clear the clothes of the upper classes'. In another context he said, 'But if I have to be reborn I should be born as an untouchable, so that I may share their sorrows, sufferings and affraits levelled at them, in order that I may endeavour to free myself and them from the miserable condition'.

Gandhiji dedicated his life fully to the service of humanity and all his workers were marked by amazing selflessness permeated by the deepest love for man. He once declared, 'I claim to love for the semi-starved paupers of India and swaraj means the emancipation of these million skeletons'.

Gandhiji was the most normal man of the modern age as a distinguished thinker observed. His love of man was so great that he did not hesitate to nurse even a leper to dress his ulcer with his own hands. While he was very busy carrying on negotiations in political matters of great moment with Viceroy at Delhi, he did not forget the poor leper at Sevagram and he was anxious to be by the side of his patient, a Sanskrit scholar suffering from leprosy.

6

INDIVIDUAL AND SOCIETY

THE RELATION between individual and society has been a mooted problem before social philosophers from Plato to Marx and from Vedic seers to Gandhiji. To the ancient Greeks, 'the state was the supreme fact of life and the efforts and actions of individuals had to flow into it just as a river flows into the sea'. The Pythagoreans taught that the individual should subordinate himself to the whole and invariably act for the general good. They agreed that since the welfare of all depended on the state, it was only reasonable to make it of primary importance. The argument, therefore, was that supporting the state would, in the end, benefit the individual. The state was a moral order and each citizen a member thereof. So much so that the theory of the city was at once ethics, sociology and economics as well as politics.

The Sophist school believed that society was unimportant in comparison with the individual men. They disapproved of state control, and thought, that government and laws were used by the weaker members of society in order to protect themselves from the stronger and more successful. Plato held that no true political life could develop without an enslavement of the individual which to totalitarian thought is tolerable, but to democratic intolerable. Plato believed that since the problem was to create a state in which all men could lead good and useful lives, the function of law was to ensure, by force, if necessary, the cooperation of the minority who would not help, of their own free will. Aristotle had somewhat similar ideas but he restricted the rights of the individual to a much greater degree.

Stoic schools held that social life was a duty before which the individual should subordinate himself. Nevertheless, they took a broad view of civilisation and declared their goal to be the good of all man-kind. The Epicureans agreed with the Sophists that the right of man should be considered first.

With the dawn of the Christian era, the same opposing theories persisted, but with a slightly different background. Those who upheld the power of state did so, in the Middle Ages, in the name of God, and, after the Renaissance, in the name of the nation and the king. The medieval schoolmen developed the idea that the state was founded by God, who had delegated his authority to the church and the King. Hobbes defended divine right of kings and said that the natural state of man was one of constant fear of attack from his enemies, to escape from which he created society. In this act, individuals, gave up many of their rights in exchange for security, and delegated power to a ruler, who, however, tyrannical he might be was a lesser evil than the terror and cruelty of their original condition. Thus, by Hobbes time, the state had become an end in itself.

Locke and Rousseau believed men to be naturally free and equal. According to them society had been set up as a contract made by the group in their common interest but even prior to this man had been naturally good and peace-loving. August Comte gave up the idea of social contract to account for the origins of society and showed that the social impulse is innate in human nature. He described the development of civilisation as taking place in three stages: military stage, revolutionary stage and positive stage. John Stuart Mill believed that some degree of State control was a necessary evil. Herbert Spencer thought that state interference should be as little as possible in order to give full play to the law of the survival of the fittest. Thus, in brief, then, there have tended to be two schools of thought on the nature of society, one claiming that the State is simply a group of individuals living together for their own mutual benefit, and the other that the State is something more.

Dr. Ramashray Roy discussed the relationship between Man and society in the following manner.

Gandhian View of Man and Society

The conception of person that sees man to be completely determined by nature, that is, by biological, psychological and sociological conditions, is unable to provide an appropriate ground for moral evaluation and political action. Once man is reduced to history and culture, his fate hangs between the oppressive poles of reductionism and determinism. And yet various perspectives on man do have some notion of human freedom. To talk of human freedom is also to talk of suppressing some or other elements of nature and rising above it. Freedom may be worthwhile in its own right, however, its real worth lies in its instrumentality, its usefulness for seeking certain substantive end - perfection, self-development and so on. In this sense, the search for freedom is basically a quest for getting release from casual determination that constitutes an important characteristic of what is called nature. The quest for freedom is indicative of the fact that while man as a physical and living being is strictly subject to natural laws, he is more than this and, by virtue of this, he is above causal determination. That is why all attempts to express and ground human freedom is naturalistic terms come to nought. Man has therefore to be treated more than a biologically, psychologically and sociologically determined being; he has to be considered as an ethico-religious entity. The notion of person, therefore, has to do with man not only as an empirical phenomenon but also as a being that seeks perfectibility.

Man as an ethico-religious principle is simply a possibility. As Nagarjuna observes: 'The sense of 'I' is at cross-roads; it has a double reference. It shares at once two orders of being, the conditioned and the unconditioned; it is at once a universalising as well as a particularising tendency. It can work as much for liberation as for bondage, it can work non-clingingly as well as by clinging.'

If the sense of 'I' traverses the path of particularising tendency, the empirical self becomes absolute bringing in its wake distinctions of 'I' and 'not-I' and treating them not as relative distinctions but absolute ones. If, on the other hand, the sense of 'I' inclines towards the universalising tendency, the empirical self is treated only as a centre of experience, a baseline from which can one begin the search for the unconditioned and the quest for the real nature of one's being. It then leads to the realisation that the ultimate nature of the conditioned is itself the unconditioned reality and that there exists an essential relatedness among determinate beings. When the sense of self incorporates an ethico-religious dimension and emphasises the necessity of development, it then becomes necessary to transcend nature and chart out a pattern of development uniquely suitable for each person. Such a perspective recognises biological, psychological and sociological realities but refuses to be bound by them. The exploration of the true nature of self is inexorably linked up with the extent to which these realities are transcended. In this perspective, man is subject to the laws of nature, to be sure, but he possesses self-awareness and is capable of creating the forms of his own existence independent of the environing conditions. It recognises the importance of certain internal transformation impinging on the process of self-development unique to man.

Gandhiji refuses to accept the empirical self as true self and, while recognising the brute in man, he calls for self-purification. For him, while man is rooted in and springs from the animal world, he has the capacity to rise above it and can, only if he so recognises and wills, set on a journey to give free play to his moral and spiritual propensity for self-development. In his view, the attributes of being uniquely human are neither fixed for all times nor immutable. He believes that goodness in man can be articulated, strengthened and perfected. Once the good in man is aroused, man can move on the path of self-realisation. He pegs this hopes on the perfectibility of human nature.

For Gandhiji, self-development is learning to be human, a learning that is characterised by a ceaseless process of inner illumination and self-transformation. It is basically an understanding of one's true being and letting that being unfold itself. Since presumably a genuine knowledge of self entails a transforming act upon the self, to know in this sense is not only to reflect and comprehend, but also to shape and create. For to know oneself is simultaneously to perfect oneself. But the self-knowledge does not depend upon the knowledge of the phenomenal world. Nor is it to turn totally inward ignoring the claims of the phenomenal world. The search for the transcendental centre must be pursued in the world of here and now. But this necessity does not imply submersion into the phenomenal. The phenomenal, the 'everydayness' is not only the point of departure but also the eventual return of any significant moral and spiritual journey. This return is not however, to lose again in the phenomenal but to reshape it, recreate it and transform it according to the law of transcendental freedom.

Recognising this as being the true orientation of personhood, it should be made clear that such a perspective does not imply any anthroprocentrism. It is rather a perspective that is transcendental, to be sure; but it recognises the necessity of seeking the meaning of life in the world of here and now. This projects an 'organismic vision' which emphasises the essential unity of existence since it sees the one reflected in all and all reflected in the one. This perception of essential unity does not, however, preclude the recognition that while everything is distinct from another. Such a perspective recognises distinctions, but not differences. Moreover, such a perspective does not mean subjectivism since there is a clear recognition that no individual has a privileged access to truth. Since truth can be viewed and apprehended from various and not necessarily compatible positions, one has to recognise the 'manysidedness' of reality.

The recognition of the manysidedness of reality within the framework of the essential unity of existence leads to the rejection of exclusivism. It recognises the essential uprightness of the many positions that can be taken to define reality. As such, many paths, many ways can co-exist. By implication, it also recognises that human phylogeny has its own structure and that it cannot be fully explained in terms of some general laws governing animal kingdom as a whole. The rejection of exclusivism also points to the fact that one must abstain from imposing one's way on others in order to preserve their integrity. Such an outlook leads necessarily to the adoption of *ahimsa* as the basic principle of 'social interaction'.

It may be argued that the recognition of the manysidedness of reality may ultimately lead to differences among persons. Such differences, if they occur, are resolvable because, in the last analysis, the perception of the manysidedness of reality is located within the transcendental centre is the same in every being eventhough the path of its realisation may diverge from person to person, the perception of difference is not likely to degenerate into ego-centric aggrandisement and imperialistic expansion. This is so because the perception of the manysidedness of reality is predicated upon a strong sense of shareability and commonality. The experience of self-development through self-transformation may be personal but it is not private precisely because such an experience resonates with the inner experiences of others. Such a perspective emphasises shareability and commonality of outlook. It underlines equality, but not uniformity since it allows for different shapes of meaning as it is perceived and manifested in different persons and contexts.

Self-transformation is an inner experience and underlines inwardness. However, it is this principle of inwardness that externalises itself once the necessity of self-transformation in the world of here and now is accepted. In Maritain's words, 'Because of the very fact that I am a person and that express myself to myself, I seek to communicate with that which is other and with others, in the order of knowledge and love. It is essential to personality to ask for a dialogue and for a dialogue wherein I really give myself, and wherein, I am really received'. This necessarily imposes the necessity of liberation not through conquest but through harmonising oneself with an everenlarging network of relationships, calling for going beyond the

restrictions of anthropocentrism. Harmony, in this perspective, becomes not only a personal aspiration, but also societal goal and cosmic ideal.

The necessity of harmonising oneself with an everenlarging circle of relationship is only the other name of integration. Such an integration becomes possible only by extending the boundary of the self, not for absorption of everything else to oneself but for giving oneself to others. Thus this extended self becomes the ground for sociality. Society then turns out to be a network of extended selves rather than a mechanical aggregate or a primacy of the person but treats him as a drop of the ocean. Also, this perspective locates humanity in a highly complex web of interdependancy.

Such a perspective projects an outlook which enfolds everything into its embrace of empathy and fellow-feeling. However, to care for the world without turning to what is immediate is an anathema in this perspective. Recognising the frailty of human nature and its attachments, such a perspective does emphasise the desirability of universalising one's basic value commitments but insists on choosing a concrete path of making it possible for the basic value commitments to be universally manifested. Such a concrete path offers itself in the principle of *swadeshi*, that is concern for immediate neighbourhood. This is, again, not an event of exclusiveness or narrow parochialism. Each individual or unit has to strike the universal concrete in terms of the milieu of its own cultural heritage. Only by proceeding from wherever we are - geographically, spiritually or emotionally can we make the integral effort needed for the progress and peace of the whole of humanity.

If self-transformation is a process that turns one inward, whose external manifestations result concretely in the basic value commitments as outlined above, then the process must start from the individual himself. Without self-effort, no amount of social reordering will yield any result. As Gandhiji says, 'In the West, when they talk of the amelioration of the lot of the masses, they talk of raising the standard of life . . . how can an outsider raise the standard, when the standard is within everyone of us? We can only strive to increase man's opportunities of realising and, fulfilling his duties and getting nearer to God'.

To increase man's opportunities of realising and fulfilling his duties and getting nearer to God will depend, on how close the social order - the arena of man's making and doing conforms to the basic value commitments, one can deduce further that an appropriate social order must be based on *ahimsa*, harmony, service, duty, *swadeshi*, self-restraint, and self-sufficient autonomous local communities that emphasise non-possessiveness, equality, non-exploitation and decentralisation of decision-making. In the words of Gandhiji, 'In this structure, composed of innumerable villages, there will be ever-widening never ascending circles. Life will not be a pyramid with the apex sustained by the bottom. But it will be an oceanic circle whose centre will be the individual always ready to perish for the villages, till at last becomes one life composed of individuals, never aggressive in their arrogance but ever humble, sharing the majesty of the oceanic circle of which they are integral unit. Therefore the outermost circumference will not wield power to crush the inner circle but will give strength to all within and derive its own strength from it. . . . No one will be the first and none the last.'

7

MEANS AND ENDS

THE PROBLEM of means and end is of supreme importance in Indian philosophy. The schools of Indian thought are deeply concerned with the testing of man and the method of achieving it. It is in this respect that Indian philosophy is distinct from modern western philosophy. Man cannot live without a metaphysics. It is the philosophy of life that makes him what he is. In India, philosophy has always had a practical aim, namely to find out the means whereby man can attain unmixed happiness.

Spiritual perfection of the individual is the ultimate end of society. It cannot be considered as a means to any other end. But, there may be many other goods such as love, money, power, fame, benevolence, etc., which ordinary persons would always try to pursue. Every individual cannot be expected to be conscious of the highest end. For such people it is necessary to devise a graded hierarchy of ends which, while satisfying their general needs will yet form an instrument for the highest end. In this sense all the activities of a society may be interpreted as the expression of values that its members respect.

Attachment to the body and the things that it wants is the root cause of all evil. Men identify themselves with bodies and fight with each other. But what seems to separate man from man does not really constitute his essence. As bodies, as senses, as *prana*, as mind, we are different. But we are none of these either separately or in combinations. We are pure spiritual beings. Spirit is one and identical and constitutes one's nature. It is not limited by time, space and causation. It is Truth, Consciousness and Bliss. The realisation of this unity of spiritual existence would remove all sense of separateness. Every individual's supreme efforts will have to be directed towards the realisation of the Real which is *Sat-Cit-Ananda*. This ideal, therefore, is common. The pursuit of this would mean happiness to all. The structure of society must be planned in such a way that the realisation of both the aims become possible and easy. The subsidiary ends will be the immediate ends of actions for the majority of people. But it is possible to make the ultimate end the basis of regulatory norms which would guide and control action in the pursuit of immediate ends.

A society, if it is to survive, must regularly fulfil the supreme value of personality. The selection of means and ends is significantly important in order that the equilibrium of society is not disturbed and that the inter-relationship of means and ends is justifiable and self-consistent. This leads us to the main problem at issue. The two opposite views are: (1) Does the end justify the means? (2) Does the means justify the end? When we say that the end justifies the means, one should understand by 'means' not something which is a part of a whole process whose culmination is called the end, but just a cause of condition which is chosen by a moral agent to bring a certain effect, and which therefore acquires a peculiar value of its own - the value that any contributor object would acquire. The means is an instrumental cause, and so there is a certain distance between the means and the end which is generally not to be found between an efficient cause and its effect. It does not mean that the means is thus always an instrumental cause. Means and ends may altogether be separate from each other. If, on the contrary, means and ends formed different stages of one process only, the whole process would stand self-justified or self-condemned, and we could not possibly talk of the end justifying the means. Intensive study is the means of acquiring knowledge but only in the sense that it is itself part of the whole process which culminates in full knowledge. The whole process is one and integral and it is difficult to say here which is means and which exactly is end, since at every stage knowledge is being acquired. The case is similar when we say that eating is the means of satisfying hunger; moral practice and discipline are the means of moral perfection; deep meditation is a means of spiritual self-realisation, etc. In all such cases, the whole process must be regarded as having value and it would be different to say what amount of value belongs to the end, what amount to the means merely. The dictum that the 'end' justifies the 'means' falls to the grand if applied to the above illustrations.

The supporters of the above dictum observe that means must be taken as an instrumental cause of a possible effect which is regarded as an end. For example, the interest of health justifies, the surgeon's knife. The interests of urgent social reforms may sometimes justify the application of drastic legal remedies to cure chronic social maladies, such as removing unbearable suffering may sometimes justify even putting an end to the life of the sufferer, as Gandhiji once put an end to the life of a calf suffering from an incurable disease. And in moral life generally it may become necessary to perform surgical operations in the interests of a higher moral development. In such cases, the means is adopted out of pure motives. Naturally the end is justified.

The problem of means and ends is an important problem in the life and teachings of Gandhiji. One of the books in which he touched this problem is 'Hind Swaraj'. When he published his book *'Hind Swaraj'*, it faced severe criticisms. Some thought that he will change his ideas shortly. But he never did so. This book contains the essential ideas for a moral and spiritual revolution. In one of its chapters he expressed his views on problem of means and ends. Though he expresses his views on political ends and the means, his ideas, on this are applicable to other spheres also. Because in Gandhian way of life, life is one, the divisions such as economics, politics, sociology, education etc., are meaningless.

Man believes that violence is the law of life. But it is not so. If violence is the law of life the human life might have extinct thousands of years ago. The very existence of human beings on earth in the midst of the terrible atomic weapons shows that the law of life is love. In some cases man may achieve a little with the application of force. Modern world believes that the happy world can be built on hatred and violence. The production of atom bombs and other terrible weapons clearly shows that man is a violent being and is believing that violence brings happiness. By evil means one cannot get good end.

Gandhiji emphasised the purity of means in every walks of life. During India's struggle for freedom he had once remarked, 'I am prepared to sacrifice everything for the liberation of my country, but not Truth and Non-violence'. This clearly shows that he was certain about the non-violent means to attain the freedom of India. Non-violence is the means and Truth is the end. He approached the problems of life in a scientific way. He conducted experiments at different places in South Africa and India. One of the problems on which he conducted experiments and said was the problem of means and end. He emphasised that the means must be pure to attain the goal.

In Gandhian philosophy, the distinction between ends and means goes away and the two are considered as constituting a continuous process, and organic whole. Gandhiji's emphasis on means is partly due to the fact that man can only strive, he cannot command results. In his own words, means are after all everything. As the means so the end. There is no wall of separation between means and end. Indeed the creator has given us control over means, none over the end. Realisation of the goal is in exact proportion to that of the means. This is a proposition that admits of no exception. According to him the means may be likened to a seed, the end to a tree, and there is the same inviolable connection between the means and the end as there is between the seed and the tree.

Gandhiji was influenced by the various schools of philosophies and different sects of Hinduism. Most of his teachings and activities were influenced by the fundamental doctrines of Hinduism. He considered the teachings of *Bhagvadgita* and the teachings of the *Upanishads* as the guiding light of life. One of the basic beliefs in Hinduism is the theory of *Karma*. This theory says that every act reproduces the results. So one has to be very careful in their thought, word and deed. The present is the result of the past and future is decided by the present. The only way out of *Karma* is selfless action. In his solution to the problem of means and ends Gandhiji follows this ancient Hindu Philosophy. *Gita* says that man must do his duty, he must not expect the results. In his national freedom struggle he led the masses to action with pure means. He was quite certain about the results. He struggled for Indian independence because it stands as an obstacle to the progress of Indians. Like any other problem, the problem of means and end is also a practical problem to Gandhiji. He experimented and experienced that the means are important than the end. He was a man of compromises. He used to change his views according to the new knowledge and insights. But there are some points and issues on which he stands strongly without any changes even the whole world opposes him. One is the end and means are related with each other and they are not different from each other.

Gandhiji's ideal seems to be the only right view of the relation between the end and the means. Good means alone can lead us to everlasting peace and progress. Past history teaches us that violence engenders violence, revenge leads to counter-revenge and a war sows the seeds of further wars. A careful enquiry will convince one of the truth that means should be compatible with the end concerned. Both should be homogeneous so as to assure that the extreme of means is itself the end. In fact the end cannot be something to be attained all at once in a distant future. The end progressively realises itself through the means, and then at each step the means itself is turned into the end.

To Gandhiji, means and ends are convertible terms. The *Upanishads* have often identified the way that leads to the realisation of Brahman with the realisation itself. The end is to achieve the peaceful and blissful state of self-realisation in end through individual and social strivings. One cannot hope to reach a moral destination by means of immoral means. It is a universal dictum that hate begets hate and violence is reinforced by violence. There can be no valid contention against the universal truth of what Buddha said: 'Anger and evil should be won by love. One should suffer and peacefully resist through love instead of answering a blow with a blow'.

Dr. Joan V. Bondurant makes a brilliant analysis of the problem of means and ends. She has suggested that traditional political theories have failed to deal adequately with the problems of means. Some have admitted defeat by uneasily relying upon techniques of violence as the only alternative in the last resort. Others have made vacant gestures in the direction of a new approach, but have thus collapsed of their own weight.

On a thorough examination of the dichotomy of ends and means it was Spengler who said that what man needs above is not only a noble end but also constructive and creative means. John Dewey has made a significant contribution to this problem. He argues that only recognition in both theory and practice that ends to be attained one of the nature of hypotheses and that hypotheses have to be formed and tested in strict correlativity with existential conditions as means, can alter current habits of dealing with social ideas whereas Dewey has called attention to the need for considering means and ends as 'two ways of regarding the same actuality' and has insisted that ends be developed with the fullest considerations of existential circumstances.

Some of the goals of Gandhiji are *Sarvodaya*, *Swarajya*, Self-realisation, meeting God face to face. All these ends are closely connected with spirituality. The means must be pure - because these ends are moral and spiritual ends. So he emphasised the moral means to attain the moral end. It is impossible to get good flowers from a poisonous tree. Like this it is impossible to get good end by bad means. This view of Gandhiji is not an invention. Aldous Huxley hold the similar view in his book *Ends and Means*. The Chinese philosopher Lao Tse recommends the similar view. He said, 'To the good I would be good, to the evil I would also be good in order to make them good. With the faithful I would keep faith, with the unfaithful I would also keep faith in order that they may become faithful'.

Gandhiji was clear in his views about the social and political ends which he was pursuing. He attempted to show that *satyagraha* is the method of transforming the nature of conflict so that it is made creative in situations where it has remained wholly destructive.

One cannot reach truth by untruthfulness. Truthful conduct alone can reach Truth. Non-violence is embedded in Truth and *vice versa*. *Ahimsa* is the means. Truth is the end. Means to be means must always be within our reach, and so *ahimsa* is our supreme duty. If we take care of the means, we are bound to reach the end sooner or later.

In *Hind Swaraj* Gandhiji gave an illustration which illustrates how the means is related with end. 'If I want to deprive you of your watch, I shall certainly have to fight for it; if I want to buy your watch, I shall have to pay for it; and, according to the means I employ, the watch is stolen property, my own property, or a donation. Thus we see three different means'. Man can always aim towards the goals. He cannot command it. He can command the means. Means is within the control of the man. In Gandhian Philosophy the means and ends are like the two sides of the same coin. They are inseparable from each other. Among the two he gives importance to the means that is non-violence. In the ultimate level both truth and non-violence will merge with each other.

BIBLIOGRAPHY

Agarwal, Shriman Narayan, *Constructive Programme for Students*, Padma Publications, Bombay, 1945.

Ambedkar, B.R., *The Untouchables*, Amrit Book Company, New Delhi, 1944.

Arunachalam, K., *Khadi Economics - A Few Aspects*, Koodal Publishers, Madurai, 1974.

Bharathi, K.S., *The Philosophy of Sarvodaya*, Indus Publishing Company, New Delhi, 1990.

Bharathi, K.S., *Socio-Religious Thoughts of Mahatma Gandhi*, Dattsons Publishers, Nagpur, 1989.

Bharathi, K.S., *Gandhi and Humanity*, Gandhi Seva Ashram Samiti, Nagpur, 1989.

Bharathi, K.S., *Satyagraha of Mahatma Gandhi*, Indus Publishing Company, New Delhi, 1990.

Bharathi, K.S., *Foundations of Gandhian Thought*, Dattsons Publishers, Nagpur, 1987.

Bondurant, J.V., *Conquest of Violence*, Oxford University Press, Bombay, 1959.

Bose, N.K., *Studies in Gandhism*, Navjeevan Publishing House, Ahmedabad, 1972.

Bose, N.K., *My Days with Gandhi*, Nishana, Calcutta, 1953.

Chand, Tek, *Liquor Menace in India*, Gandhi Peace Foundation, New Delhi, 1972.

Charles, K.J., *Total Development : Essays Towards Perspectives*, Vikas Publishing House, New Delhi, 1983.

Dasgupta, S., *A History of Indian Philosophy*, Vol. V, Cambridge University Press, London, 1965.

Dhawan, Gopinath, *The Political Philosophy of Mahatma Gandhi*, Navjeevan Publishing House, Ahmedabad, 1962.

Diwakar, R.R., *Saga of Satyagraha*, Gandhi Peace Foundation, New Delhi, 1969

Dube, S.C., *Indian Village*, International Library of Sociology and Social Reconstruction, London, 1955.

Dutta, D.K., *Social, Moral and Religious Philosophy of Mahatma Gandhi: A Critical Analysis*, Intellectual Book Corner, New Delhi, 1980.

Fridlander, Walter, A., *Introduction to Social Welfare*, Prentice-Hall of India (Pvt) Ltd., New Delhi, 1963.

Gandhi, M.K., *Non-violence in Peace and War*, Volume I, Navjeevan Publishing House, Ahmedabad, 1962.

Gandhi, M.K., *Constructive Programme and Its Meaning and Place*, Navjeevan Publishing House, Ahmedabad.

Gandhi, M.K., *Social Service, Work and Reforms*, 3 Volumes, Navjeevan Publishing House, Ahmedabad, 1941.

Gandhi, M.K., *Economics of Khadi*, Navjeevan Publishing House, Ahmedabad, 1941.

Gandhi, M.K., *From Yeravada Mandir*, Navjeevan Publishing House, Ahmedabad, 1945.

Gandhi, M.K., *Hind Swaraj*, Navjeevan Publishing House, Ahmedabad, 1946.

Gandhi, M.K., *Women and Social Injustice*, Navjeevan Publishing House, Ahmedabad, 1945.

Gandhi, M.K., *Basic Education*, Navjeevan Publishing House, Ahmedabad, 1951.

Gandhi, M.K., *Communal Unity*, Navjeevan Publishing House, Ahmedabad, 1951.

Gandhi, M.K., *Satyagraha in South Africa*, Navjeevan Publishing House, Ahmedabad, 1950.

Gandhi, M.K., *To the Students*, Navjeevan Publishing House, Ahmedabad, 1949.

Gandhi, M.K., *Towards New Education*, Navjeevan Publishing House, Ahmedabad, 1953.

Gandhi, M.K., *Removal of Untouchability*, Navjeevan Publishing House, Ahmedabad, 1955.

Gandhi, M.K., *Khadi - Why and How?*, Navjeevan Publishing House, Ahmedabad, 1955.

Ganguli, B.N., *Gandhi's Social Philosophy Perspective and Relevance*, Vikas Publishing House, Delhi, 1973.

Gregg, R.B., *Economics of Khaddar*, Navjeevan Publishing House, Ahmedabad, 1946.

Homer, A. Jack, *Religion for Peace*, Bhartiya Vidya Bhavan, Bombay, 1973.

Iyengar, A.S., *All Through the Gandhian Era*, Hind Kitabla Ltd., Bombay, 1950.

Iyer, Raghavan N., *The Moral and Political Thought of Mahatma Gandhi*, Oxford University Press, Oxford, 1978.

Jhingan, M.L., *The Economics of Development and Planning*, Vikas Publishing House, New Delhi, 1979.

Jones, E. Stanley, *Mahatma Gandhi. An Interpretation*, Holder and Stoughton, London, 1948.

Kantouzky, Detlf, *Sarvodaya the Other Development*, Vikas Publishing House, New Delhi.

Kumarappa, B., *Why Prohibition*, Navjeevan Publishing House, Ahmedabad, 1952.

Kumarappa, J.C., *Gandhian Thought*, Vora and Co., Bombay, 1951.

Louis Fischer, *The Life of Mahatma Gandhi*, Bharatiya Vidya Bhavan, Bombay, 1955.

Louis Fischer, *A Week with Gandhi*, George Allen and Unwin, London, 1943.

Mahadev Prasad, *Social Philosophy of Mahatma Gandhi*, Viswa Vidyalaya Prakashan, Gorakhpur, 1958

Mashruwala, K.G., *Towards Sarvodaya Order*, Navjeevan Publishing House, Ahmedabad, 1971.

Mathur, V.S., *Gandhiji as an Educationist*, Metropolitan Book Co. Ltd., Delhi, 1951.

Migabraim, U.S., *Message of Mahatma Gandhi*, Publication Division, Delhi, 1969.

Nanda, B.R., *Gandhi and His Critic*, Oxford University Press, Delhi, 1985.

Ostergaard, Geoffrey, *Non-Violent Revolution in India*, Gandhi Peace Foundation, New Delhi, 1985.

Patil, V.T., *Studies on Gandhi*, Sterling Publishers, New Delhi, 1983.

Pyarelal, *Mahatma Gandhi: The Last Phase*, 2 Volumes, Navjeevan Publishing House, Ahmedabad, 1958.

Pyarelal, *Towards New Horizons*, Navjeevan Publishing House, Ahmedabad, 1959.

Radhakrishnan, *Mahatma Gandhi: 100 Years*, Orient Longmans, Delhi, 1968.

Rajendra Prasad, *Constructive Programme: Some Suggestions*, Navjeevan Publishing House, Ahmedabad, 1942.

Ramashray Roy, *Gandhi: Soundings in Political Philosophy*, Chanakya Publication, Delhi, 1984.

Ramashray Roy, *Self and Society : A Study in Gandhian Thought*, Sage Publications, New Delhi, 1984.

Ramjee Singh, *The Relevance of Gandhian Thought*, Classical Publishers, New Delhi, 1983.

Sethi J.D., *Gandhi Today*, Vikas Publishing House, Delhi, 1978.

Srimali, K.L., *The Future of Basic Education*, Panjab University, Punjab, 1966.

Tandon, Viswanath, *Selections From Vinoba*, Sarva Seva Sangh Prakashan, Varanasi, 1965.

Tandon, Viswanath, *The Social and Political Philosophy of Sarvodaya after Gandhi*, Sarva Seva Sangh Prakashan, Varanasi, 1965.

Tolstoy, Leo, *The Law of Love and the Law of Violence*, Rudolph Field, New York, 1948.

Unnithan, T.K.N., *Gandhi and Social Change*, Rawat Publications, Jaipur, 1979.

Varma, Viswanath, Prasad, *The Political Philosophy of Mahatma Gandhi and Sarvodaya*, Lakshmi Narayan Agarwal, Agra, 1972.

Verma, I.B., *Basic Education: A Reinterpretation*, Shri Ram Mehra and Co., Agra, 1969.

Vinoba, *Essence of Basic Education*, Sarvodaya Pracharlaya, Tanjore, 1967.

Vinoba, *Shanti Sena*, Sarva Seva Sangh Prakashan, Rajghat, 1963.

Vinoba, *Thoughts on Education*, Akhil Bharat Sarva Seva Sangh, Varanasi, 1959.

INDEX